Advice for Successful Families

Advice for Successful Families

THE CHRISTIAN FAMILY TODAY

Fr. Alain Delagneau

2915 Forest Avenue | Kansas City, MO 64109

French original entitled *Conseils pour réussir une famille chrétienne aujourd'hui*, a special issue of *Marchons Droit*, No. 24, 2008. © 2008 Abbé Alain Delagneau

©2013 by Angelus Press
All rights reserved. No part of this book may be reproduced or transmitted in any form or by any means, electronic or mechanical, including photocopying, recording, or by any information storage and retrieval systems without permission in writing from the publisher, except by a reviewer, who may quote brief passages in a review.

ANGELUS PRESS
2915 FOREST AVENUE
KANSAS CITY, MISSOURI 64109
PHONE (816) 753-3150
FAX (816) 753-3557
ORDER LINE 1-800-966-7337
www.angeluspress.org

ISBN: 978-1-937843-21-2
FIRST PRINTING–July 2013

Printed in the United States of America

Contents

Preface	vii
The Sacrament of Marriage	1
The Harmonious Union of the Spouses	9
Conjugal Love: Its Friends, Its Enemies	25
Catholic Education	33
Some Family Virtues	43
May Catholic Spouses Consider Separation?	73
The Spiritual Life of the Home	79
Human Equilibrium	93
Friends or Enemies of the Christian Home	97
Conclusion	105
Appendix: Consecration of Families to the Sacred Heart of Jesus and the Immaculate Heart of Mary	107

Preface

In founding His Church, Christ took into account the distinguishing social aspect of man. That is why He instituted two sacraments of a social character: matrimony and the priesthood. We do not receive these sacraments firstly for ourselves, but for the good of society.

The sacrament of marriage is ordained to the propagation of the Mystical Body of Christ, to the increasing of the number of the adorers of the Blessed Trinity. The family is the basic unit of Christian society, which has for its mission co-operation in the formation of the Catholic city of heaven.

The priest himself has the mission to conduct all men to their eternal destiny. The Mass is at the heart of this mission: by it, he renders to God, with the participation of the faithful, a cult worthy of Him, and the graces of salvation and sanctification which they need. By his preaching and his spiritual counsels, he enlightens souls with the light of God. By the sacraments, he gives divine life to the faithful in abundance. By his authority, he unites the faithful around the unique Savior of the world.

For more than forty years, all the forces of evil have combined to corrupt and destroy Christian society from beginning to end. In order to do so, they have attacked the priesthood and the Christian family. The priest has lost his reason to exist, his specific vocation. From that moment, the Faith and the Christian spirit have been disappearing and souls lost. The family, since 1968, has lost its traditions, its Christian focal point, in married life as well as in the upbringing and education of children. This is why divorce or separations are rampant, and children are steeped in the liberal and sensual spirit in which they are plunged.

What can be done? What can be proposed to rectify this situation? We must form saintly priests and saintly families!

This booklet has no other ambition than to explain some fundamental principles to help you to succeed in the context that is ours. It is a strict duty which each home must make its own: to form a family that is united and virtuous, bringing forth good fruit before God and man. A successful Christian family is one from which the good God can draw forth holy vocations. It is essential often to have this thought in mind, and this from the most tender years until the maturity of the souls entrusted to you.

I wish to present to you some concrete aspects of family life, because it is often more effective to do so than to recall general principles. This is, therefore, a document to read and to re-read regularly so that your lives might be instilled with a truly Christian spirit. Everything written here is important!

As soon as one is united in the bonds of marriage, one must sanctify oneself, as well as one's spouse, by means of life in common and by the reception of the sacraments. Do not hesitate to offer this work to your friends, to newlyweds, and even to those who are engaged. Each must often consider the ideal towards which he strives.

As you will notice, the chapters are not of equal length. This is because I wanted to emphasize family virtues and the spiritual lives of the spouses. However, human aspects of family life are not neglected. Grace is grafted upon nature!

May the Blessed Virgin and St. Joseph bestow light and grace in abundance upon the readers of this booklet.

Feast of Christ the King, 2008

The Sacrament of Marriage

Definition

Marriage is a natural institution of divine origin. God created human beings male and female, and He deposited in them the instinct to procreate and to populate the earth. "Be fruitful and multiply and fill the earth" (Gen. 1:28).

Marriage can be defined thus: "Marriage is a contract by which a man and woman legitimately give each other the perpetual and exclusive right to the acts necessary to the procreation and upbringing of children, and to the aiding of life in common."[1]

Note well that marriage is a contract of a particular kind. It is not a matter of a task to accomplish or of goods to be exchanged. It comprises the totality of the person. It involves the whole person. Each one gives oneself voluntarily and forever, and each one depends on the other. And each one has the proof—founded on the love of one's spouse—that this dependence is not a diminution of oneself, but a perfection.

The essence of marriage resides in the reciprocal gift of the right of conjugal relations. Community life (shared roof, bed, and board) belongs to the integrity and not the essence of marriage. Subsequently, Our Lord elevated marriage to the dignity of a sacrament. In his catechism, St. Pius X defined marriage this way: "Marriage is a sacrament instituted by Our Lord Jesus Christ that establishes a holy and indissoluble union between man and woman and gives them the grace to love each other in a holy way and to bring up their children in a Christian manner."

---

[1] Msgr. Martin.

St. Thomas Aquinas specifies: "Marriage is life in common regulated by divine and human law."[2]

The Goods of Marriage

Theologians, according to St. Augustine, uphold three goods of marriage:

- the "*bonum prolis*": the generation and upbringing and education of children;

- the "*bonum fidei*": conjugal fidelity and mutual support;

- the "*bonum sacramenti*": the grace to fulfill the duties of Christian marriage, to attain mutual sanctification through life in common, and to educate one's children in a Christian manner.

The *Bonum Prolis*

The primary end of marriage is the procreation and the education of children. To divert the conjugal act from this end by natural means (for example, by incomplete acts) or by artificial means is always gravely sinful: "Since the marriage act is by its nature destined to the begetting of children, those who, in its accomplishment, deliberately apply themselves to take away its strength and its efficacy, act against nature. They do a shameful and intrinsically dishonest thing."[3]

The primary end of marriage is, therefore, the procreation and education of children: "Among the goods of marriage, children hold the first place.... Christian parents must understand that they are not only called to propagate and conserve the human race on the earth ... but to give sons to the Church, to create citizens, saints, and

---

[2] Suppl., Q. 44, A. 3.
[3] Pius XI, *Casti Connubii*, 1930.

friends of God, to the end that the population of Christians increases day by day."[4]

Marriage is called in Latin *"matrimonium,"* which comes from *"mater"* or "mother," because a woman marries above all to become a mother. What is marvelous is to understand that God wanted to make spouses "pro-creators." He wanted to associate them in His act of creation. This extraordinary end well merits being privileged by connection with personal interest: "Marriage, as a natural institution, in virtue of the will of the Creator, has for its primary and intrinsic end, not the personal perfection of the spouses, but the procreation and the education of new life. The other ends, all and equally willed by nature, are not ranked with the primary end, and still less are they superior, but essentially subordinate."[5]

We take the opportunity here of calling to mind the magnificent prayer of the young Tobias which he uttered before taking his wife to himself: "O Lord, God of our fathers, Thou who didst make Adam from the slime of the earth and didst give him Eve as a companion, Thou knowest that it is not for a base passion that we enter into marriage, but the sole love of posterity who must bless Thy name, forever and ever" (Tob. 8:9).

The *Bonum Fidei*

The secondary end of marriage is the mutual help of the spouses and the remedy of concupiscence. From the beginning of creation, God said to Adam: "I will give him a helpmate similar to himself" (Gen. 2:18). Man is in need of affection, exchanges, counsels, support in trials and the exercise of virtue. All of that is offered to him in faithful common life: two complementary beings helping each other in the way of human and supernatural life throughout their married life!

---

[4] *Ibid.*
[5] Pius XII, 1951.

In His infinite bounty, God willed to grasp all that is the noblest, the greatest, in the human heart: the love which unites two complementary beings, in order to form the basis of this common life, of this mutual perfection. Each owes the other to guard and nourish their love and their esteem for each other in order always to be a help to each other in the way of perfection.

If the children leave home around the age of twenty-five, the spouses dwell with each other for their whole lives. It is, therefore, a privileged means in the path of sanctification. The love of the spouses has priority over the love of the children!

Life in common facilitates not only material and spiritual life, but it is also a remedy for concupiscence, in easing the desires of the flesh: "But for fear of fornication, let every man have his own wife: and let every woman have her own husband. . . . Defraud not one another, except, perhaps, by consent, for a time, that you may give yourselves to prayer: and return together again, lest Satan tempt you for your incontinency" (I Cor. 7:2-6).

The marriage debt exists in order to aid the spouses from falling into sin. One spouse cannot refuse a reasonable request for conjugal relations by the other. It is a grave duty because by the marital contract one does not belong to oneself any longer: "Let the husband render the debt to his wife: and the wife also in like manner to the husband. The wife hath not power of her own body: but the husband. And in like manner the husband also hath not power of his own body: but the wife" (I Cor. 7: 3-4).

The *Bonum Sacramenti*

St. Pius X tells us in his catechism, "The sacrament of marriage signifies the indissoluble union of Jesus Christ with Holy Church, His spouse and our most loving mother." One sees from this to what loftiness, to what dignity is elevated the sacrament of marriage! St. Paul makes explicit this vocation of the spouses to "represent" noticeably the union of Christ and the Church when he says, "Husbands, love your wives as Christ also loved the Church and delivered Himself up for it. . . . Let women be subject to their husbands as to the Lord" (Eph. 5:22-25).

Among Christians, one marries to become a saint. To do so, it is necessary to enter into the plan of God. What a sublime ideal, but how demanding for the husband! He must unceasingly pursue the natural and supernatural good of his spouse, and that to the point of sacrificing himself, that is to say, his selfishness, his own spirit, and his own will. He has received graces in order to mold himself after Christ in His love for the Church. Christ gives the example, teaching, organizing, consulting, sustaining, and saving His Church.

As for the wife, she also has a marvelous vocation. She is the partner of her husband. God has instilled in her an influence of soul so powerful over the heart of a man in order to help him to realize his calling to be conformed to Christ, as well as the submission to realize together the common work of the sanctification of the children and familial harmony.

The Catechism of St. Pius X adds: "The sacrament of marriage gives an increase of sanctifying grace and confers special grace to fulfill faithfully all the duties of the married state." Pope Pius XI clarifies:

> This sacrament, when no obstacle is placed in the way, not only augments sanctifying grace, the permanent principle of supernatural life, but adds, as well, particular gifts and good-hearted gestures, the seeds of grace. It elevates and perfects natural strengths, to the end that the spouses are able not only to understand by reason but intimately to sense and hold firmly, to want to efficaciously put into practice and to accomplish all that relates to the married state, to its ends and its duties. It concedes to them, finally, the right to the help of actual grace each time they need it to fulfill the obligations of their state in life.[6]

Spouses cannot sanctify themselves as do simple faithful! They are in the married state. They must, therefore, sanctify themselves in this state of life, but they have also the right to actual graces in order to practice the virtues of their state: charity, fidelity, pa-

---

[6] *Casti Connubii.*

tience, mercy, conjugal chastity, the wisdom and strength to raise their children well, respect and obedience. In order to receive and to profit from these graces, the spouses must confess often and ask in prayer, especially in Holy Communion, the help of which they stand in the greatest need to accomplish their role in a Christian manner. Let us observe that the prayers of spouses made in common are more perfect and more meritorious than prayers said individually. They pray then for the end that the spouses become the living image of the union of Christ with His Church, which is definitely the mystery of the most perfect charity.

The Properties of Marriage

The state of marriage has two essential properties: unity and indissolubility.

Conjugal Unity

Conjugal unity is the union between one man and one woman. God said to Adam at the time of his creation: "Man will leave his father and mother, and will attach himself to his wife, and the two shall be as one" (Gen. 2:24). Our Lord calls to mind this law and adds: "Whosoever shall put away his wife and marry another committeth adultery against her, and if the wife shall put away her husband and be married to another, she committeth adultery" (Mk. 10:11-12).

Indissolubility

Just as the Word is united with His human nature and the union of Christ and His Church is forever sealed, so is the sacramental union of man and woman indissoluble. The indissolubility flows from the unity; as they are one sole unit, they cannot be separated. "Man and woman form but one sole body. That is why they are no longer two, but one sole flesh. Just as it is criminal to mutilate a man, it is equally criminal to separate a man and woman who are united by the marriage bond."[7] "What God has joined together, let no man put asunder" (Mt. 19:6). It is God who has fixed the terms of the contract of marriage and of the spouses. Even by common agreement, it cannot be broken.

The fact that Catholics cannot for an instant envision divorce obliges them to practice the most beautiful Christian virtues in the face of difficulties more or less serious. Just as Christ will never abandon His Spouse, the Church, in spite of all her faults, so the spouses cannot imagine breaking the conjugal bond that unites them for life.

---

[7] St. John Chrysostom.

The Harmonious Union of the Spouses

Preliminary Considerations

We live in an individualistic society, and too often we reason and function in our own little world. The Catholic—in order to live fully the grace of his baptism—has a higher view, that of God. He views and considers his family as a member of the Mystical Body of Christ, which is animated by grace from the Head; that is to say, from Christ. He permeates himself with the laws which rule the life of the Mystical Body of Christ in order to conform himself to it. Each Christian spouse understands what his place is in the plan of God and examines himself to determine if he is fulfilling his role.

In a few words, let us recall what order is: the hierarchy willed by God for the formation and perfection of the Mystical Body of Christ.

Christ in His human nature is at the same time submissive to His Father and the Head of the Church. By His complete obedience to His Father, He collaborates perfectly with the merciful plan of God. His submission comprises all His nobility, all grandeur, all the treasures of His life. He has obtained for us an eternal redemption, and "God also hath exalted Him and hath given Him a name that is above all names" (Phil. 2:9). Christ in His human nature is equally Head of the Church. By this title He teaches, nourishes by His grace, and commands and requires obedience from His Church.

The priest is the second link in the chain. He is also submitted to an authority, the Vicar of Christ. At the same time, he is leader of his parish and of his priory.

The husband is the third link. He is submissive to the priest of his parish for his doctrine. As well, he likes to consult him in important decisions which touch upon the moral and spiritual life of his home. He is at the same time head of his family and responsible for the souls which compose it.

The wife is the fourth link. She is submissive to her husband and thus collaborates in the development and perfection of the members of the home. With her husband, she shares in the directing of the education of the children and in the exercise of authority over them.

The children complete this hierarchy. They sanctify themselves by obedience to their parents and, therefore, by the respect that is due to them.

What is marvelous to notice is that Our Lord in His human nature belongs to the two extremities of the chain and unites them. He was a child, living in obedience vis-à-vis His earthly parents—"He was subject to them" (Lk. 2:52)—and at the same time, He is Head of the entire Church.

This Christian view of things helps us to escape from false ideas which destroy order in the family and which come to us from the French Revolution. We can no longer associate inequality with inferiority. God desired in society a variety of roles and, therefore, an inequality in view of the harmony of the whole. This hierarchy has a complementariness of functions, but it is clear that a child can be as holy as his father or mother. This is the beautiful example given us by Our Lord.

Along the same lines, obedience does not result in the atrophy of a person but in his enrichment, since we are dealing with the order of supernatural virtues. The greatest saints who most transformed the world lived in obedience. Far from being degrading, this virtue allows God to act more profoundly in us.

We consider next the family as a society. It need not be invented. It suffices to enter into the plan of God, who created not only man and woman, but who conceived equally marriage and the laws of marriage. Man and woman are two different and complementary beings. This is why their morphology, their psychology, and their role in the bosom of the home are different and complementary.

If each has the humility to accept the function that is his within the home, a good foundation is laid. Each spouse is considered as a complement indispensable to the equilibrium and the perfection of the home. Following upon that, neither any longer envisions a life alone, whether it concern his duties of state, his relaxations, pleasures, trials, piety, or sanctification. Many use the term, "my other half."

As in society at large, God wished to invest one of the spouses with authority. In the family, it is the husband. One cannot change this plan of God without introducing a grave disorder for the spouses as well as for the children. Children need to see in the details of daily life this order willed by God in order to be able to reproduce it one day.

Humility, which is the foundation of all Christian life and of all human society, allows us to see the beauty of this order. It consists in accepting, loving, and living fully the place granted us by the good God.

The Head of the Family

According to the will of God, the father possesses the authority in the bosom of the family and therefore has the responsibility before God and man for his family. Here are a few duties of the head of the family:

- He will often call to mind that his authority is delegated to him and that therefore he will one day have to render an account of his management. "The head of all men is Christ" (I Cor. 11:3). This is why he will often study the Gospel, meditating upon it in order to acquire the spirit of Our Lord.

- He will make it a habit to consult the priest on delicate questions disputed in his family. This reference to the Church is willed by God and can reassure the wife and the children, who understand that his decisions are not arbitrary.

- He will pray for the souls entrusted to him. He will be

able to support especially in prayer, alongside the Divine Master, each of those committed to him.

- He will realize that alone, he is nothing and that alone, he can construct nothing solid. This is why he will place all his efforts in realizing a harmonious union with his spouse. Without this unity of spirit, his efforts will bear little or no fruit.

In order to arrive at this goal:

- He will take the time to speak with his spouse about his projects and the cares of the family. He will listen to suggestions from her and will explain his objectives, bearing always in mind the principle at stake.

- To make headway, the two will share the same spirit in such a way that neither spouse ever utters a complaint against the other in front of the children, and that the children thus sense the unity of the parents. Of course, it is up to the husband to make the ultimate decision and to implement the practical means to its realization.

- He will easily praise his wife for her collaboration and good initiatives. By valuing his wife, then, the husband will assure himself of a precious and devoted help. He will leave to his wife a great latitude in the domain that is hers: the keeping of the house and the preparation of meals with the expenses which accompany it.

- He will be an artisan of family peace in the image of Our Lord. This is why he will regulate family conflicts in a calm and just manner, as did St. Louis.

In order to do this, he will:

- Never openly oppose his wife in front of the children. In weakening her authority over them, he will weaken his own at the same time.

- Find a way, when it is a matter of trifles, to ease tension by speaking of something else, by joking, or by proposing a game.

- He will (in private) correct disorders which arise in his wife or among his children.

It is not an easy task! However, eradicating bad habits with kindness and firmness avoids greater conflicts. Cowardice and impatience in this domain cost dearly. They can be the occasion of coldness, oppositions, and yelling.

The following disorders affect all domains of family life: lack of a schedule, disorder in the house, extended telephone calls, a spirit of criticism and of mockery, the wearing of immodest attire, dangerous friendships, and idleness.

The husband participates in the working of Divine Providence, and he has duties which follow upon such participation:

- He will have the desire, the care, to do good to those souls entrusted to him, all the while respecting order and justice.

- He is the religious leader of his family. He is careful to maintain the schedule of family prayers, the reception of the sacraments, and he gives the example by his presence when it is possible. The too frequent absence of the father from family prayers lessens the importance of this act and is always detrimental to the children.

- He is responsible for his children's souls and, therefore, for the increase of virtue and of family qualities among them. He encourages reading that is good and cultural. He provides a good formation for their souls, thereby protecting them from errors and from all that can soil their souls: TV, unmonitored Internet usage, bad magazines.

- He is protective of their bodily lives, ensuring that they are balanced, and use their free time well. He mercilessly throws out video games, which destroy attention, concentration, and the peace of mind of children.

- He watches over the social and cultural life of his family, as well as over exterior devotions. He protects his home from the bad influences of the world.

- He concerns himself with the work of helping to restore Christian society. This is a duty of the head of the family, since his children will be influenced by society and will live in society. With generosity but also prudence, he will see what he can do, along with others, to reduce corruption in ideas and morals, to paralyze the action of the enemies of the Faith and to reconquer society for Our Lord.

  In this field of action, the head of the family will recall that alone, he is nothing. He needs the encouragement of his wife and the co-operation of his friends beneath the undisputed authority of a leader who possesses both strength and prudence. The noblest enterprises, without profound unity centered on a competent and respected authority, are doomed to failure.

Let us summarize the **qualities** of the head of the family which favor obedience: God the Father is characterized by goodness. Such is the primary quality of the head of a family. Goodness facilitates the opening of hearts and the exercise of authority. Goodness and kindness are not signs of weakness, but of understanding and care for the good of each. This goodness is expressed in slightly different ways and adaptations, but not in a concession of principles.

The father of a family will regularly practice the virtue of prudence. This virtue consists in looking for good solutions, drawing upon his experience and the advice of his wife, and then deciding the best solution. In the end he must put into effect his resolution, either personally or by delegating it to someone who can and will.

He will know how to sacrifice his selfishness, his comfort zone, and his own interests for his wife and family. "Husbands, love your spouses as Christ also loved the Church" (Eph. 5:25). We know how much Christ loved the Church, to the point of sacrificing Himself for her. He will be available to listen to and to encourage others in their family tasks. He will know how to give compliments. It is very stimulating when encouragement comes from authority.

He will take care to remain worthy of the respect of his wife so that she will be proud of his engagements, his attitudes, and of his qualities.

Towards the children, the father of the family will cultivate kindness and firmness. The child must sense that his father loves him and that he does not just favor the child's whims but truly desires his good. The father will be also vigilant and available. He will know how to guess his children's weaknesses in order to help them, always ready to listen to them and spend time with them. Finally, he will not forget that his children need to be proud of their father by reason of his qualities, his business, his culture, and of his good fight for the Faith.

Let us take a look at the **consequences of the faults** of the father of the family.

- If the father is harsh and abrupt in his authority, not knowing when to listen to his spouse or to his children, he favors a spirit of questioning and of rebellion, whether exterior or interior. Much will be done and said behind his back, and the souls confided to him will not sanctify themselves. Perhaps his children will even drift away from the Faith or fulfill their duties in a bad way by a spirit of opposition, of rebellion, or of flight.

- If the father is insignificant, making no demands and fleeing responsibility, the wife will take his place, attempting to supply for his deficiencies, and there will be disorder. As a result, when the wife departs from her mission, the boys will lack character, strength of soul, and a sense of responsibility. All too often, for the sake of peace, the mother will give up in the face of certain demands, and laxity will install itself among the children, a laxity which will prepare them for all possible falls in the world at large.

- If the father does not know how to organize, to command precisely, he will always be unhappy because nothing will get done, or what is done will not be done well. In addition, some will lack a spirit of sacrifice in their work. Reproaches, acts of impatience and of anger will then appear and harm the souls in the family on account of their injustice. The command not having been clear enough, everyone does as he pleases.

- If the father of the family gives a bad example, being the authority of the family, he greatly harms the souls of the children. A father who no longer practices the Faith or who only comes to say prayers complaining drives piety from the souls of his children. A father who spends much of his time in front of the Internet makes his children selfish. A father who has a spirit of criticism, mocking everyone, will have children of the same bent.

Fortunately, with the grace of God, there are beautiful exceptions to these principles, but they remain exceptions!

The Collaborator of the Head of the Family

The wife, after the preceding exposé, has the right to say as did Esau to his father, Jacob: "My father, have you reserved a benediction for me also?" (Gen. 27:36). And God responds to her: "Yes, I have reserved for you a magnificent part also, because through you I think of the most holy Virgin who is 'blessed among all women.'" The wife has a mission certainly different, but complementary to that of her husband in the accomplishment of one work: the formation of a family worthy of heaven.

The Submission of the Wife

Before speaking of her own mission, let us recall the plan of God: the sub-mission, in reference to her husband: "Women, be subject to your husbands as to the Lord" (Eph. 5:22).

In order to fulfill her own vocation, the wife must fully accept this plan of God. To dispute with him or to submit with bad grace is to endanger the equilibrium of the home and the perfection of the members of the family. It is a disorder. Submission is not a dishonor or a sign of inferiority. It is an expression of a great and noble virtue: obedience, obedience to God through human authorities.

Today we have lost the esteem of this virtue because it is in fashion, now more than ever, to follow one's own will. This attitude is in direct opposition to the way of sanctification. In the Our Father, we say: "Thy will be done." In this prayer consists our perfection: to know and to practice the holy will of God.

But where do we discover the will of God? We find it in His Commandments, His counsels, but, also, in authority. God has given to the head of the family a participation in His own authority. It is a fact.

The wife must do everything to find the will of God rather than impose her own. A wife who is desirous of perfection will love to receive orders, counsels from her husband, and will accept them as coming from the Lord whether they are agreeable or not.

> And you, wives, lift up your hearts! Do not be content with accepting and barely submitting to the authority of your spouses, to whom God has submitted you by the dispositions of nature and of grace. In your heart-felt submission, you must love the authority of your husband, loving him with that respectful love which you bear towards Our Lord, Himself, from whom descends all the power of the leader.[8]

---

[8] Pius XII, September 10, 1941.

Of course, the husband, being a prudent man, will always ask counsel of his wife and will take her opinions into account. However, it is up to him to make the final decision. Pope Pius XI specifies that the obedience of the wife only extends to what is good, and sometimes, she must entreat her husband:

> This submission, besides, does not deny that, without abolishing the freedom which rightly reverts to the wife....It does not command her to bend to all the desires of her husband, no matter what. She can and must resist when his will is not conformed to reason or to the dignity of the wife....
> ...If the husband fails in his duty, the wife must supply for the direction of the family. However, for what concerns the very structure of the family and its fundamental laws established and fixed by God, it is never permitted to overturn or undermine them.[9]

Finally, to end this delicate subject, let us say, in practice, the reciprocal love of the spouses reduces to a minimum more often than not the exercise of marital authority. Confiding in one another, they harmonize and naturally unite their minds and wills to make identical decisions in view of the common good.

What should be done when classic subjects of discord present themselves: for example, the upbringing of the children, the choice of schools, company keeping, expenses for the management of the house, visits of in-laws?

In the first place, one must know how to calmly explain one's point of view, and then listen to that of the other, to try to enter into his thoughts; to recognize the need to ask counsel of a trustworthy person. Then it is up to the husband to make the decision in view of the common good, knowing that he will be responsible before God for his choices. The wife will then submit herself, not reluctantly, but in a spirit of Christian docility to the will of God.

We come to the vocation proper to the wife and mother of the family. I will summarize it by two comparisons. Just as the Holy Ghost is the soul of the Church, the wife is the soul of the home, the

---

[9] *Casti Connubii.*

heart of the home. She is the ray of sunshine which rejoices souls and makes them attain maturity.

The Wife Is the Heart of the Home

Just as the Holy Ghost moves souls and the Church interiorly, the wife has a vocation completely interior, full of discretion, but oh, how noble and necessary! She has the power to animate the members of the family, to elevate them by virtue of her shining charity. She is the heart of the home, as the Holy Ghost is the Spirit of love in the Blessed Trinity. Without love, there is no true life and no harmonious development of life. Love can, on the contrary, give rise to beautiful gifts of self. It is helpful to cite the example of St. Therese of the Child Jesus, who understood her mission in the bosom of the Church, as the wife must realize her mission in the bosom of the home:

> To be your spouse, O Jesus! To be a Carmelite! To be, by my union with Thee, the mother of souls, all that should be sufficient for me. However, I sense in myself other vocations: I feel the calling to be a warrior, a priest, an Apostle, a doctor, a martyr....
>
> I would like to accomplish all these most heroic works. It seems I have the courage of a Crusader. I would like to die on a field of battle for the defense of the Church.
>
> The vocation of the priest! What love, O Jesus, would I bring to Thee in my hands when my voice would cause Thee to descend from Heaven! With what love would I give Thee to souls! But, alas, in desiring to be a priest, I desire and would have need of the humility of St. Francis Assisi, and I feel the calling to imitate his refusal of the sublime dignity of the priesthood. How to reconcile these contrasts?
>
> I would like to enlighten souls like the prophets and the doctors of the Church. I would like to travel the earth, preaching Thy name and planting Thy glorious cross on infidel soil, O my Beloved! But one only mission will not suffice for me. I would like at the same time to announce the Gospel in all parts of the world, even to the remotest isles.
>
> I would like to be a missionary, not just for a few years, but I would like to have done so from the beginning of the world until the end.
>
> But above all, I would like to be a martyr. A martyr! Such is the dream of my youth. This dream has grown with me in my little cell of

Carmel. But there is another madness, since I do not desire only one sort of torture. I must experience all of them. . . .

As Thou, my adorable Spouse, I would like to be scourged, crucified. . . .

I would like to be skinned as was St. Bartholomew, to be plunged in boiling oil as St. John. I desire, as St. Ignatius of Antioch, to be ground by the teeth of wild beasts, in order to become a bread worthy of Christ. With St. Agnes and St. Cecilia, I would like to present my neck to the sword of the executioner, and like St. Joan of Arc, in a flaming pyre, to utter the name of Jesus!

If my thoughts are concentrated on unheard of torments which will be the part of Christians in the time of the Antichrist, I feel my heart quiver. I would like these torments to be reserved for me.

Open, my Jesus, Thy book of life, where are reported the actions of all the saints. These actions I would like to accomplish for Thee!

To all my ravings, what will Thou respond? Is there in the world a soul smaller than mine? However, because of my weakness, Thou wouldst be more willing to gratify my infantile desires, as Thou desirest to gratify today other desires greater than the universe. . . .

These desires become a veritable martyrdom. I opened one day the epistles of St. Paul, in order to find some sort of remedy for my torments. My eyes fell upon Chapters XII and XIII of the first letter to the Corinthians.

The Apostle explains that all the most perfect gifts are nothing without charity, that charity is the most excellent way to go surely to God.

Finally, I found rest!

I understood that if the Church had a Body composed of different members, the most necessary, the most noble organs would not be missing. I understood that It has a heart, and that this heart was burning with love. I understood that love alone gave movement to the members, that if love came to be extinguished, the Apostles would no longer announce the Gospel and that martyrs would refuse to spill their blood for the Faith.

I understood that love contains all vocations, that love is everything, that it embraces all times and all places, because it is eternal!

So in my excess of delirious joy, I cried: "O Jesus, my Love! My vocation, at last I have found it! My vocation is love! Yes, I found my place in the bosom of the Church, and this, O my God, Thou hast given to me. In the heart of the Church, my Mother, I will be love!

Thus, I will be all; thus, my dream will be realized!"[10]

In order to be filled with divine charity and to spread it, the wife must have a spiritual life, an interior life well-nourished. It is imperative for her not to neglect it! Each day, she must go drink from the source of charity by a heart-to-heart talk with God. She will also love to pray frequently to the Holy Ghost. "Come, Holy Ghost, fill the hearts of Thy faithful. . . ." The wife will be vigilant, therefore, in her words, her actions and her counsels, always to be guided by a love for souls.

If the wife is to be the heart of the home, it is because by her entire nature she is ordained to receive and to develop life, that life which is a work of charity. This is why, in church, she wears a veil which reminds her of her great vocation. She is like a tabernacle, the receptacle of divine life, which is covered with a veil to remind us that we are before a great mystery of charity. There is represented the nobility, the dignity of the woman, and she must be proud to wear this veil which manifests to the eyes of men and angels the excellence of her mission.

The Wife Shines as the Sun

The rays of the sun have two active principles: they illumine and they make all things move. One finds these qualities in the wife. She makes the home and family life pleasant. The wife gives a soul to the family nest by her harmonious taste. She renders the house agreeable by the order and cleanliness which reign there.

God has filled woman with such qualities that she is attentive to detail and order. Her welcoming and loving smile gives to everyone the desire to return home. When the mother is absent, something essential is missing for everyone.

The heart of the queen of the home goes all out in the celebration of feasts and holidays by the preparation of pleasant meals and decorating the house. She spends herself as well without measure, with all

---

[10] *Story of a Soul*, Ch. 11.

her heart, when one of the members of the family is in pain. She suffers almost more than the one who is suffering.

In every case, she imitates the Blessed Mother, who gave such joy to Our Lord by her presence, her attentions, her thoughtfulness, and which love and concern she communicated to Him so profoundly in His sufferings during His Passion.

The wife also has a particular art for helping her husband to give the best of himself. She knows how to set about reminding him and encouraging him in his family duties. In the trials which occur, she shows herself strong and of a fighting spirit, often lifting the morale of her husband. Her natural joyfulness, her smile, helps him to rise above his worries. Her retirement from the world permits her to be supernatural and to more easily turn souls towards God.

The mother also has the mission and the qualities to form and to educate, to bring up, the children whom she has borne in her womb. She has an intuitive side which helps her to foresee change in her child in order to intervene in time. This intuition makes her guess his pains and temptations. She has an observant side which permits her to see the needs of each child. Her great sensitivity and natural love will go even further and will open the hearts of her children to her so that they will love to confide in her. Her unfailing patience will permit her to continue this work of education which is ongoing. Her mercy and her spirit of sacrifice will make her forget her pains, her disappointments, and to pursue the sometimes thankless work of education. Her tenacity, finally, helps the child to persevere in his good efforts in order to acquire good Christian habits.

Pope Pius XII justly said: "The wife, the mother, is the sun of the family. She spreads around her light and heat. . . . Her look and her word penetrate sweetly into the soul, soften, soothe, and appease the tumult of the passions and remind man of the joy of well-being and of family life, after a long day in the office."[11]

Let us end by considering some **essential qualities** of the wife:

- A wife will sanctify herself in marriage by applying

---

[11] March 11, 1942.

herself to realizing more and more her beautiful and noble vocation.

- First of all, this constant devotion to all—which all too often is unrequited—demands much self-abnegation. She does good by loving, and takes no account of the rest. It is there that is found the purity and nobility of the heart. To begin to look at herself or to complain is to distance herself from her vocation. A good mood, a habitual smile, and constant availability have their price!

- Having this vocation to help souls to blossom, she must possess sweetness and patience. Never is she disturbed, discouraged, or irritated. To attain such peace, she is careful in how she plans things so as never to be stretched too thin, if she can help it, and never too tired. If need be, she plans rest or relaxation in order to always give the best of herself.

- Set apart from the world, she cultivates piety and modesty so as to elevate souls and to attract the graces of the Holy Ghost upon herself and upon her family. This supernatural role is of the greatest importance and must translate itself into her lucid look of charity.

- Sometimes, the wife only thinks of doing good to others and exhausts herself. She needs to be recharged in her natural life, as well as in her spiritual life. To take time for herself (relaxing activities, meditation, retreats, and so on) is not time stolen from the family. On the contrary, it is time well spent in order to fulfill her vocation more efficiently.

Let us demonstrate **the consequences**, sometimes tragic for the home, of a wife who **does not fulfill** her role:

- If the wife is worldly, lazy, selfish, a spend-thrift, many things will be neglected and everyone will suffer.

- If the wife yells all the time, is nervous and high-strung, the sun will be lacking from the home, and souls will not open up and confide in her.

- If the wife engages regularly in useless gossip, she exposes herself to scandal, to superficiality, and to the wasting of time.

- If the wife is touchy and sensitive, she very quickly fosters a stifling and unpleasant atmosphere in the home.

- If the wife is authoritarian and independent, a bad spirit will penetrate the home and hearts will not open up.

- If the wife lacks piety and self-sacrifice, a solid foundation of a good Christian life will not be imparted.

- If the wife is possessive, the children will be spoiled and over-protected. They will become fragile when confronted with the spirit of the world.

In practice, when there are familial failures, the responsibility of the wife is generally predominant. At the same time, successes in the home are in large part due to her influence and contributions to the family.

Conjugal Love: Its Friends, Its Enemies

Man is a creature of God, who lives in eternal charity. He is made to love and to be loved.

The distinguishing characteristic of love resides in the giving of the best of oneself to another. This love is accompanied by joy and perfection. It is found in maternal love, paternal love, and in friendship. What is marvelous is that God grasped what is the most beautiful, the sweetest in the human heart—love between two beings, two complementary beings—to serve as the foundation of the sacrament of marriage.

This love extends right to the union of the body in view of procreation. That is to say, it incarnates, in some way, and it naturally espouses, or "marries," the laws of the Creator: unity and indissolubility.

However, over time and with the manifestation of faults of character, there can be a certain wearing down, a certain coldness which develops in this feeling of love. In addition, it is capital to understand that marriage does not have a time limit, but it plants a solid foundation for the increase of mutual love which will help the spouses to grow in virtue, one towards another. It is essential, therefore, to apply oneself to nourishing and developing this mutual love.

How to Cause This Link of Love to Grow

We must not forget that with the grace of baptism, and even more, with the grace of the sacrament of marriage, this love is one of charity. It is a participation in Divine Love. This is why it is a duty for the spouses regularly to ask the Holy Ghost to increase in them their charity, their love, so that they will draw ever nearer in manifesting the love of Christ for His Church. Regular confession and communion will greatly aid in the increase of mutual charity.

Conjugal life is life given into the heart of each of the spouses. It must be cultivated by exterior attitudes which at the same time actualize the love which each one proves for his spouse and exquisitely affect it. These are the gestures of tenderness, the compliments, the affectionate words, the dedication expected by the other, the gifts which are unlooked for or which are given to solemnize special feasts, and privileged moments together.

The natural inclination of charity is kindness. Each of the spouses must be careful to continue to do good to his spouse, to make Christian life easy and agreeable. This is why it is necessary to remain vigilant of the needs of the other, to be attentive to veiled complaints, to fatigue, to circumstances when the other is overwhelmed with work or worry.

When one spouse learns that the other has not finished the rosary, he offers to finish it with the other. If one is in desolation or suffering from an obvious temptation, the other suggests praying with him and increases his attentions to the other. If one is given to complaining, the other listens for a minute and then suggests that the trials be offered in unison with the work of Redemption.

True love is demanding. It looks to help those around it to become always better, in the rhythm that is their own. Here is what one husband proposed to his wife:

> Your love without demand pushes me to mediocrity;
> Your demands without love paralyze me in my efforts;
> Your demands without patience annoy and harden me;
> Your demanding love helps me to be better.

Common life requires numerous small sacrifices or renouncements in order to keep peace. The Mass reminds us that true charity does not consider the sacrifice required of self. It is the most beautiful expression of charity on earth. All sacrifice of self is a communion with Christ.

Charity is full of patience and mercy in the face of small disappointments and contradictions, as well as of the faults of one's spouse. Charity supersedes all these things in bearing wrongs patiently, accepting them, and offering them up. Acceptance is the necessary point of departure. If one makes a mistake, irritation and then anger will soon appear. One spouse cannot change everything about the other. He or she must know how to be demanding on one point and flexible on the others!

Love aspires after the union of souls. Love has need of intimately knowing the spouse in order to realize a profound union with him. That is why confiding in each other is so necessary. Some people need to be helped and encouraged in order to reveal their inmost thoughts. For others, confiding in one's spouse is easier. However, reciprocity is indispensable in order to progress to a true union. The evening or outings together lend themselves more to these precious moments.

At Mass, Christ manifests daily all His love for His spouse, the Church. He expresses it perfectly by His sacrifice, by Communion, and by the gift of His presence. Spouses also need a "real presence" to one another in order to maintain their mutual love. It's not only a matter of a physical presence where each has his own occupations, but of a presence which permits ordinary conversations. Common work in the house or with the children, or better yet, games together, remain good occasions for diverse conversations and attention to one another. The spirit of each spouse must remain free of his worries and of his work in order to be available for the other!

Enemies of Conjugal Love

Inordinate Affections

This is the case when the wife gives all her time, all her expressions of affection, to her children, and the husband is left neglected or abandoned. This is a grave disorder! At the same time, the husband can throw himself into his job and bring his work home, leaving his wife alone, so much so that his house becomes a hotel for him.

Sometimes, one of the spouses does not know how to say no, which is why he is always absent from home during prayer time, neglecting his duty.

The love of the world is another great danger for the spouses, because in the world is found only appearances, superficiality, putting up a front, and human respect. The socialite is a slave to the spirit of the world and of the reproaches of the world, which are opposed to the Christian spirit. "He who wishes to be a friend of the world makes himself an enemy of God" (Jas. 4:4).

Selfishness

In this disorder each looks for tranquility, comfort, and pleasures, in turn. This fault destroys love because one spouse ceases caring for the good of the other. One may let himself be captivated by sports, the other by television, surfing the Internet, or by reading. Another will find satisfaction in games played alone, catalogs, or endless telephone calls. Silence begins to reign in the home. Everyone is still together, but everyone is in his own little world.

Uncorrected Character Flaws

Little by little, these faults become habits for the spouse who makes no effort to correct them. These are such things as pessimism, messiness, being too demanding in details, continual yelling, lack of generosity, having an authoritarian side, being overly sensitive, stubbornness. In the face of a lack of progress, the husband or wife becomes discouraged and distances himself little by little. Prudishness in the expression of one's feelings can equally upset one of the spouses, resulting in the cooling of his own feelings.

Conjugal Relations

Let us remember here again that in their conjugal relations the spouses must not do anything to prevent the fulfillment of the primary end of marriage, which is procreation. That would be a grave disorder! The selfishness which excludes children, and, therefore, the law of God, will soon become selfishness between spouses and will be the beginning of a lack of balance in the heart of the home.

Therefore, those spouses sin mortally who use natural or artificial means to prevent conception (incomplete acts, onanism, sterilization, contraception, or IUDs). Pius XI made this very clear:

> As some depart manifestly from Christian doctrine such as it is transmitted from the beginning and always faithfully kept . . . the Catholic Church, rising up in the midst of this moral ruin, greatly raises her voice by our mouth, as a sign of her divine mission, in order to guard the chastity of the nuptial link sheltered from this stain and promulgates anew that the whole usage of marriage, whatever it be, in the exercise from which the act is deprived by artificial means of its natural power to procreate life, offends the law of God and of nature, and that those who have done the same are stained with a grave fault.[12]

Stripped of impurity or selfishness which seeks its own pleasures, conjugal relations are a real treasure for the spouses, a passing summit of the expression of their love. They therein express all their tenderness, their gentleness, their gift of themselves, their union of heart, hoping to conduct the other to the profound happiness of all it can be according to the plan of God.

These relations strengthen their mutual attachment and cause little familial tensions to disappear. They also learn renouncement and discipline so that each arrives at pleasure at the same time. This act, which one can call sacred because it regularly consecrates the love of the spouses, is willed by God and must be realized by charity, that is to say, for the glory of God and the good of the spouses.

The primary end willed by God, which is to transmit life in order to people the heaven of the elect, can never be positively excluded by an incomplete act or contraceptive means. The secondary end remains, even in periods of sterility of the wife. God willed it thus for

---

[12] Pius XI, *Casti Connubii*.

the good of the spouses: to appease concupiscence, to strengthen mutual love. It is good, therefore, to use marriage at all times.

However, it is necessary to watch that the flesh does not dominate the spirit, that is to say, that the attractions for the pleasures of the flesh do not supplant, little by little, the love of the will of God and of the good of the spouse. One could fall into the selfishness which leads very quickly to sin and then to grave sin by onanism.

That is why, as in all things, it is necessary to work towards moderation in marital relations. Throughout the year, they can be spaced out or even ceased by mutual agreement, as during Advent and Lent. Their union will become, then, more spiritual and, therefore, stronger. Tenderness, far from disappearing, becomes more profound, more spiritual, and holier. However, it is greatly necessary that the progress be common and full of charity.

On the other hand, it is always necessary to watch that conjugal relations be dignified, imprinted with respect, gentleness, and consideration. Always seeking for new techniques in order to attain maximum pleasure chases away purity of heart and plunges itself in selfishness, which is the number one enemy of conjugal love. "Even in the legitimate pleasure which the Creator Himself destined in the usage of the instinct of generation, Christian spouses must know how to maintain themselves within the limits of a just moderation."[13] Otherwise, he who lets himself go to undignified limits only exacerbates concupiscence, and instead of finding a remedy, opens the door to desires that are increasingly disordered.

We arrive now at the question which many parents ask us after the third or fourth child: may one continue to use marriage whilst at the same time limiting relations to the infertile periods in the woman's cycle in order to space out children? Let us remember, firstly, that a large family is a blessing for the home and for the Church. Large families are most often united families in which there are plenty of opportunities for developing a Christian spirit.

---

[13] Pius XII.

The deliberate and exclusive use of the infertile periods, called Natural Family Planning, can at times be permissible, in order that the secondary end of marriage be fulfilled when it is morally impossible to fulfill the primary end. Pope Pius XII in his 1951 discourse to midwives indicated the four reasons that could justify this rhythm method: health of the mother, eugenic and social reasons, and poverty. However, these must be grave reasons that make it irresponsible to have a child at that particular time. Moreover, many of them only apply temporarily. Since it is very difficult to judge in one's own case, and possible to fall into sin by using this method without sufficient reason, then a confessor or spiritual director should be consulted before using NFP, bearing in mind the great blessing of children and the stupendous result of the *"Fiat"* of the Blessed Virgin Mary when confronted with a pregnancy that she had not planned. The spacing of children for convenience' sake is certainly not a sufficient reason. Nature frequently takes cares of this, since the nursing of infants most of the time suppresses ovulation.

Catholic Education

We are not concerned here with covering all the details of a good Christian education. However, we must be realistic. Our youth, in the traditional Catholic movement, frequently do not evince the nobility of the education imparted to them. We must admit, in fact, that they demonstrate many disorders—attractions for the world, estrangement from Tradition, immaturity, imprudent and fragile marriages, and a loss of the sense of the combat for the Faith. The good fruits that we have before our eyes are in proportion to the sacrifices of the parents who, in general, choose good schools. Nevertheless, these are the young families that have the mission of restoring Christian society! This is why it is good for us to reflect upon certain aspects of education which have been neglected.

The advantage of all crises is that in facing them we return to the foundation of our virtues and deepen that foundation. A father and mother should simply make us think of the characteristics of God the Father and of the most blessed Virgin Mary in the educating of our souls! Together, they form Christians in the image and resemblance of their Divine Son, guided by the same love, the same Holy Ghost. For them, each soul is unique. They combine goodness and strictness because it is a matter of forming saints. The harmony of their action is infallible.

Such is the model of Christian parents! The natural and supernatural love of the parents must be evident. The child must truly feel their love in a unique way and believe that they desire his good. They must know how to make time for him and to adapt themselves to him. From the moment that he is assured of their love, he will accept the demands they make of him, to the extent that they are explained and to the extent that they lack harshness.

In addition, the unity of action, the harmony of the parents in their children's education, must be without flaw. If one is more lax than the other, it destabilizes the children and makes them start questioning authority and becoming lax.

To summarize the suggestions I want to make after showing what sort of spirit must animate the spouses, I will rely upon the presentation that Our Lord Himself made: "I am the Way, the Truth, and the Life" (Jn. 14:6).

"I am the Way"

Our Lord gives the example of a certain number of essential virtues. Parents educate firstly by their example.

The Respect of God and of Parents

The Second Commandment commands us to respect God and His holy name. It is very important for everyone in the family to pronounce the sacred names of Jesus, of the Father, and of the Holy Ghost, with deference, bearing in mind that we are speaking about or to Divine Persons who have the right to great consideration by reason of their perfections and of their goodness towards us.

In the same spirit, parents need to explain to their children the respect owed to one's parents and to authority figures, due to the authority which has been delegated to them by God, to their wisdom which has been acquired by experience, and to their dedication to their children's well-being. This respect expresses itself in the manner of speaking of and to one's parents. Parents must never criticize a priest or teacher in front of their children, even if they believe him to be in the wrong.

Prompt and Joyful Obedience

This virtue is the most indispensable for progress in the Christian life. The child must learn to love obedience through the examples set by Our Lord, Our Lady, and of the saints. By each act of prompt obedience, the child is enriched with virtue and grows supernaturally.

Very often, parents explain the beauty of this virtue and give an example, while explaining, "The priests say. . . ," "Dad asks." Of course, in order to be obeyed, parents must not give orders constantly, but with discernment. On the other hand, they must never tolerate disobedience. The child must realize that his parents have his well-being at heart, even if he does not understand their methods. Authority must be exercised with calmness, with a firm tone of voice, and by precise orders.

Anger and yelling are absolutely forbidden. When a child disobeys, there must follow a swift punishment according to the age of the child, his fault, his temperament, to which parents should later add an explanation in order to educate the child.

The Spirit of Sacrifice

Surprisingly, in his first years, the child is able to do difficult things easily for God and his parents. This is the proof of grace growing within him. However, there will be more difficult pathways and more arduous spheres of action as he grows older. Caprice, or following one's whim, quickly becomes ingrained and begets many sins. In addition, it is necessary to show the child the beauty of the attitude which allows him to escape from the slavery of his own will and to make his soul grow in the love of God. One can use the times of Lent and Advent to suggest sacrifices and to propose new efforts in some area for a particular intention.

Promptness in rising and in completing one's studies is essential, as well as discipline in arranging one's things, keeping the family schedule, and respecting habitual devotions. Boarding school does not dispense children from their regular chores around the house. Also essential is accomplishing one's duty of state, which is a matter of persevering in the same work, even if tedious, in order to persevere later in the active life.

Working on a farm or with the land is very educational because it demands persevering effort, but at the same time offers the consolation of seeing the fruit of one's labor.

In addition, it is important to encourage the child by explaining to him that his soul is strengthened and ennobled with beautiful virtues by repeated sacrifices on his part.

The supernatural motive of helping to save souls and to deliver poor souls from purgatory can help to encourage certain children.

The Love of Purity

Many children regress in virtue because impurity takes a greater and greater hold on them. The flesh dominates the spirit, and all disorders follow upon this regression. The child must be formed by his parents in this domain, according to his age and in a simple and supernatural manner, so that bad conversations or looking at bad images (pictures, people, movies, etc.), do not dominate him.

The love of purity, with the love of God and of the Blessed Virgin Mary, bypasses all the horrors of mortal sin. As regards impurity, the child must understand that he must never put himself in the occasion of this sin because any sin of impurity is always very serious. He must turn away—his eyes, his body, and his thoughts—in order not to be stained by sin, and he must pray to the Immaculate Heart of Mary to maintain his peace. There are, of course, bad companions to fear, but also bad images, posters, worldly attitudes, idleness, and nighttime. It is good to retire in the evening with the reading of the life of a saint and a rosary in one's hand. The love of Our Lord and of the most holy Virgin will help tremendously in the preservation of purity of heart.

Please allow me to evoke an image which may help: St. Paul tells us that we are temples of the Holy Ghost. The Holy Ghost resides in the summit of our souls, and before this holy tabernacle, there is also the altar of our heart from which arises the sacrifice of ourselves, but also acts of love which honor His Divine Majesty. This supernatural reality must help us to keep our thoughts and desires pure knowing that we are always in the presence of God.

Joy in the Family

In order to blossom and to continue to give oneself generously, the soul needs profound joys. True joy follows effort. If everything is easy, if the child is helped too much, he will be familiar with sensible pleasures but not profound joy, which is to be found in advancing in virtue and in being victorious over temptation. Such, therefore, is the importance of having material, spiritual, and intellectual projects— re-doing a room in the house, eliminating swear words from one's vocabulary, studying life in the Middle Ages.

There is also to be found a great joy in profound spiritual conversations among the family. This deepening, which is the fruit of exchanges and personal reflections, procures for each great satisfaction. Simple relaxation with the family affords still greater joys, because therein is experienced a reconciliation and a union of hearts. Each child should also have a center of interest, a hobby, that will help him to overcome difficult moments. These family joys will help the child, at the appropriate time, not to distance himself from the family circle (by an immoral life or a bad marriage).

"I am the Truth"

Our Lord came to earth to enlighten our minds and to teach us how to live the Faith.

Having Convictions

The youth, the child, assumes the doctrine of his parents. Later, when he is confronted by the world which will destabilize him, it is then that he will have need of personal convictions. To have them, he himself must have studied important subjects of current interest. Teaching does not suffice, nor does reading. Studying requires taking up a pen, reflecting upon arguments, and summarizing them.

The father himself can play the "devil's advocate" to help his children to get to the bottom of things, to the heart of the argument. This intellectual work is indispensable today, and too few young people do this sort of thing!

On the other hand, the youth must realize that it is not their personal ideas that they are defending, when it is a matter of doctrine, but the Eternal Truth which cannot change, any more than can the honor of Our Lord Jesus Christ. This will explain the firmness and inflexibility of their convictions.

The Fighting Spirit

The world in which our young people are living and growing up is lax and liberal. What they must fear above all is this worldly spirit, which causes people to marginalize their convictions in order not to displease the world. If one is afraid of differentiating oneself from the world, of being criticized, or seen badly, one will not persevere in the Christian life. Following upon lukewarmness, there will be a general relaxation of principles and convictions in one's life.

Young people must understand that it is a grace to live today with the spiritual and intellectual richness which they have received in Catholic Tradition. It is up to them to elevate their souls with a good will rather than letting themselves be degraded by concessions which, once begun, will never end.

May they remember these words of Our Savior: "You are the salt of the earth. But if the salt loses its savor, wherewith shall it be salted? It is good for nothing but to be cast out and trodden upon by men. You are the light of the world. A city seated upon a mountain cannot be hid. Neither do men light a candle and put it under a bushel, but upon a candlestick, that it may shine to all that are in the house. So let your light shine before men that they may see your good works and glorify your Father who is in heaven" (Mt. 5:13-16).

The illusion consists in not wanting to be different from the world and not wanting to oppose and denounce current doctrinal and moral evils. Let us well understand that he who does not fight is drawn into error and evil. One is also kidding oneself if one has good ideas and expresses them, but lives like everyone else regarding dress and use of free time. The light of truth and the example of virtue must shine brilliantly together!

Good Friendships

We are not interested in forming anti-social, solitary young people! It is indispensable for the young to have good friends with whom they can enjoy serious conversations and healthy pastimes. The influence of a friend is very important, above all, in difficult moments. Parents must watch out for the friendships their children form and the get-togethers they wish to frequent.

Sometimes the influence of an adult whom the adolescent admires will be a determining factor in his perseverance, which is why the choice of godparents is very important, as well as the friendship between the child and his godparents.

"I am the Life"

Our Lord has come to give us a participation in His Divine Life, and He wants this life to grow within us over the years.

Openness of Heart

"I am meek and humble of heart" (Mt. 11:29). Our Lord has come to conquer hearts, which is why He is invested with all virtues.

Parents have a role similar to that of a spiritual director regarding their children. They must be careful, therefore, to gain their confidence so as to facilitate giving them counsel, encouraging them, and regaining them, if need be. To do this requires being readily available, as well as being gentle and sensitive to the child's needs, and having a true love for their souls. But the resulting gain is well worth the effort!

It is around the ages of eight or ten that one must begin to work in order to follow up with that foundation in adolescence and the years in which great decisions will be made. Some children will find confiding in their parents easier than others. However, without irritating those who do not find doing so very easy, the parents must guess their thoughts and trials in order to help equally each type of personality. These things must be done in a natural manner outside of an activity or an event.

The Sacraments

It is especially when we prepare ourselves well for the reception of the sacraments and make a good thanksgiving afterwards that Our Lord increases His virtues in us.

Our children need to be helped to frequent the sacraments and to understand their importance in the spiritual life. Parents must be careful to give motives of contrition and to help form concrete resolutions. Next to penance, they should teach their children not to forget to thank God and to be aware of the joy of a profound purity of heart. Of course, they will ask Our Lord with confidence to help them to keep their resolutions or ask the advice of the priest.

Parents must receive Holy Communion, not just the children. They must desire these visits to have the joy of adoring, thanking, and praying to our sweet Savior. He comes to us because He loves us and wants to transform us into Himself, to fill us with His graces, and to augment in us the life of virtue. It is the moment to reveal to Him our weakness, our littleness of virtue in this or that regard: "O Jesus, I am lazy in getting up in the morning. Give me the grace to get up each morning with joy and promptness."

Daily Prayer

It may seem that this is an impossible resolution to keep. The truth is that children are entirely capable of concentrating upon an image, reflecting upon it, and praying. They just need to be taught how to do so. Their souls need, just as do ours, this profound and intimate friendship with the good God! St. Theresa of Avila defined prayer by these words: "It is the conversation of a child with God, his Father." Subsequently, children can be given a book like that of the Eucharistic Crusade or a "Thought for each Day" by a saint.

Perseverance in this five- or ten-minute daily prayer will bear unsuspected fruits. Children will thus learn to make the connection between their daily lives and their supernatural lives. They will depart from a purely practical religion to enter into a truly spiritual life.

Let us add that boys are not to be educated as girls are. It is necessary to have in mind the qualities and virtues each must possess in order to fulfill his proper mission.

Relations with Children That Have Gone Astray

Let us conclude by considering a sad question with which certain parents are unfortunately confronted: "What must we do if one of our children is living in sin (living with someone outside of marriage)?" Of course, firmness is necessary on the part of both parents in order to protect the other children from this bad example. At the same time, parents must try to keep in touch with the prodigal child in order to help him escape from his disorder.

In principle, do not receive the one living in sin into your home. As far as the child living in sin is concerned, he is received in the family to the extent that he is not strengthened in his sin but is helped to escape from it. The whole family must pray for his conversion and return to a good Catholic life. The advice of a local priest is indispensable in order to maintain a Christian attitude.

Some Family Virtues

Spouses who are solicitous for their sanctification and that of their children will love to reflect often upon and to examine themselves on their practice of Christian virtues. They will take care as well to help their children to acquire a love and practice of these same virtues.

The liturgical year is a good supernatural occasion to exercise as a family the practice of a particular virtue. One can also, each month, pay particular attention to one of the others' virtues. What is important is not to neglect any of them, so that your spiritual life grows in a harmonious manner.

After presenting quickly each virtue in a certain order, I will give you some suggestions which seem to me essential. Rather than following the usual order of presenting the virtues, I will follow an order which seems to me the most practical and which will permit me to lay a solid, profound, and stable foundation for the spiritual life. This chapter is long, in view of the importance of the subject. Feel free, therefore, to read it many times.

Putting these suggestions into practice will create a climate in the home that is conducive to the fostering of good vocations and the formation of future spouses who are profoundly Christian. These counsels also permit the spouses who follow them to sanctify themselves in family life and by family life.

The Spirit of Faith

The Faith teaches us to believe all the truths that God has revealed to us and that the Catholic Church teaches us. This Faith must transform our lives, since by this virtue, we see everything in the light of

God, and we know God both in His personal life and in His perfections. St. Paul tells us, "The just man lives by faith." He sees and judges everything according to God.

Our lives, our occupations, the people we run into, the events in which we take part, the things we possess, the sins we commit or notice in others, everything then takes on its proper dimension. Our supernatural outlook refocuses it all, because behind tangible appearances, we identify God in His divine presence, His action, His holy will, and in His judgment. It will be easily understood that this supernatural outlook facilitates a virtuous, united, and happy home life.

Now, some examples.

It is important to remember that everything we do is done beneath the eyes of God, for God, and so that it may be meritorious for heaven. Whether it concerns our professional life, the upkeep of the home, the life of a student—all our efforts (for the soul in a state of grace) prepare for us an eternal recompense.

So why are we thrown off by criticism, difficulties, lack of recognition, and by failures? Does not the importance of all we do reside in doing it for God and by God, that is to say, in asking of Him the grace we need for each moment? It is necessary to bear this in mind, especially when we are fighting complaining, discouragement, or any sort of sadness.

The eyes of faith also make us regard the members of our family in a supernatural light. Behind their faults, there is an extraordinary reality: they are children of God, and the good God asks me to co-operate with His grace in helping them to become better. How can I refuse His request? He has confided these souls to me in such a way that, with His grace, I might help to embellish and enrich them. Remembering this calling will change my attitude towards them. I will then be inclined to have respect, kindness, and patience towards them.

The Faith also teaches me that I am a temple of the Holy Ghost as long as I remain in a state of grace. This reality obliges me, in respect to my body, to maintain dignity in my attitudes and words, and still more in my heart, not giving entrance to thoughts of rash judgment, hard feelings, or anger.

Living the Faith in the context of family life easily helps us to overcome all sin. We must all protect our souls from the enemies of God! The spirit of faith also inclines spouses and children to enjoy Christian and supernatural conversations with each other. These are chances to reflect upon and to deepen the teachings which they have heard or read about.

Without frequent Christian conversations, we lose our reference to the Faith. This is serious because we risk having a compartmentalized Christianity, limited to exercises of piety. It is not easy, in the naturalistic world in which we find ourselves, to live with a Christian spirit throughout the day. It is very helpful to have conversations on Catholic topics or from a Catholic point of view.

The Faith also helps us to see sin from a different angle. The sin of one's spouse, of one's children, is firstly an offense committed against God, which should incline us to suffering and offering reparation. Considering sin from this viewpoint, we will find words or penances to help this or that member of the family to regret his sin and to correct it.

Sin also gives a bad example to or scandalizes others. This example very quickly rubs off on those around us. Sin all too often begets sin. Vicious gossiping engenders still more vicious gossip, anger engenders more anger, laziness engenders more laziness. Reflecting on this aspect, each member of the family will make a real effort to change.

Finally, the spirit of faith permits us to understand and, therefore, to experience either pleasant events or sufferings in a Christian manner. Understanding events allows us to thank God or to exercise the virtues of patience, resignation, confidence in God, or the correction of our faults.

God is Providence. Nothing escapes Him, and by His all-powerfulness, He rules everything. "For those who love God all things work together unto good" (Rom. 8:28), St. Paul tells us. Following upon that knowledge, it is up to us to profit from everything that happens to us, and to help the other members of our family to do the same.

All these examples show us how much a Christian family that lives the Faith can sanctify itself. Each member helps the others to rise above a too human or a too selfish view of people or of events.

Humility

One of the most intolerable things in a family is the presence of any form of pride, whether it be self-importance, ostentation, stubbornness, sensitiveness, independence, or its many other forms. Humility dismisses this obstacle and affords a disposition which attracts both divine and human blessings.

In the modern world, pride and the cult of self are nourished from childhood, making a unified and peaceful family life very difficult. Pride must, therefore, be pursued and destroyed by the constant practice of humility.

Humility is linked with the cardinal virtue of temperance. Each of us bears within himself two feelings: self-esteem and the desire to be esteemed by others. Original sin causes these sentiments to degenerate into pride. Temperance suppresses complacency with one's self, with one's own spirit, with one's own will, and the disordered desire of being praised and honored.

Two habitual attitudes will help us to live in humility: a more realistic knowledge and acceptance of our limits and of our weaknesses, and an ease in humbling ourselves in the face of the good that we do or the qualities that we have. St. Teresa of Avila said, "Humility is truth."[14] Humility of heart makes us increasingly aware of our nothingness, of our lack of being able to do anything good, and of our constant state of being a sinner. Humility of heart helps us to accept this reality.

The parable of the Pharisee and the publican is very instructive. All too often, we fixate on the faults, real or imagined, of other mem-

---

[14] *Way of the Interior Life*, 6:10.

bers of the family and compare their qualities to ours! Because of this, we lack the mercy and charity needed to help our neighbor to correct his faults. This pride fosters anger, coldness, and hurtful words. It also makes us self-righteous. We must return to reality! Who are we? Sinful creatures!

As long as we are creatures, we do not know everything, and there is always room in us for improvement. The qualities, responsibilities, or authority that we have freely received are to be cultivated for the benefit of others, but do not give us in any case a reason for superiority. We will have to render an account: "Give an account of thy stewardship" (Lk. 16:2).

As long as we are sinners, we must nourish in ourselves a spirit of contrition and of compunction. St. Paul tells us, "Serving the Lord with all humility and with tears . . ." (Acts 20:19). This habitual contrition must lead us to have patience, forbearance, and mercy towards our neighbors' faults. The one prayer of the Ave Maria, "Pray for us sinners," should maintain us in these dispositions.

As long as the creature is a sinner, advice, reproaches, or even injustices at the hand of those around him, must be received with peace as he looks all the while to derive profit from them.

We now come to the necessity of humbling ourselves. Our Lord sets a constant example of this for us from His birth to His death. Let us, therefore, have the desire to humble ourselves with Him, as He humbled Himself, remembering these words of the Gospel: "He who humbles himself shall be exalted" (Mt. 23:12). Let us love not putting ourselves first. Let us also love asking advice of our spouse and giving credit to the counsel he gives us.

However, since we are attempting to give a formation to the children and to unite the spouses, it is good to state simply that we must eliminate self-seeking from the good actions that we might be able to accomplish in the course of the day. Let us also love to praise others for their good qualities and noble efforts and to recognize our faults (in a discreet way, if it is in front of the children). A family in which each person applies himself to practicing the spirit of faith and of humility rests upon a solid foundation. Charity can blossom to the extent that the spirit of sacrifice is also present.

The Spirit of Sacrifice

There is no Christian life without sacrifice, and there is no Christian family that will bear good fruit without regular sacrifices.

We live in a world that is lax and liberal. In practice, it denies original sin and its consequences. It also constantly encourages us to let ourselves go. Instead of elevating ourselves above our disordered passions, the world incites us to follow them, to achieve so-called fulfillment and happiness.

We who are Catholic know that all the world's suggestions are folly and lies! The path of our perfection—the Beatitudes—was traced out for us by Our Lord in His preaching and in His Passion. We must simply follow Him as all the saints have done.

Each morning, let us gaze upon our crucifix for a moment in prayer. Let us hear Our Lord tell us again and again, "It is by the Cross that I atoned for sin, and it is by the Cross that I manifested to you My sublime virtues. Are you not going to put them into practice this day in order to make it Catholic? Look upon Me often, and I will help you."

These few motives will help us to maintain a constant spirit of sacrifice, to make reparation for our past sins, to avoid committing new ones, to deny ourselves in order to make it easier to exercise virtue, and to offer penances to God to beg Him to help us.

Penance and Mortification

The Church, during the time of Lent, asks us to do penance in order to repair the damage caused by our sins. Why not plan some penances that will be accepted by everyone in the family, in order to purify all its members, so that the whole family will receive an increase of faith and charity? Here are some examples: making the Way of the Cross on Friday, fasting on Friday, no dessert on Saturday (with the funds saved, have a Mass offered for the souls in purgatory), not letting anyone complain about his health without necessity, practicing prompt obedience in union with Jesus in His Passion, showering in cold water.

All spiritual authors tell us of the necessity of mortifying our senses in order to avoid sin. The fruit of these sacrifices is seen very rapidly. Our tongue and our eyes are what cause us most frequently to fall into sin. We must also limit the amount of time we spend on the telephone, visiting with the neighbor, and in our evening conversations. What a waste of time and what occasions of sin! Let us make sure we fulfill our duties while always keeping a sense of the sociable.

We must keep custody of our eyes, turning them away from all that will hurt us (immodest outfits, billboards, advertisements, the Internet). By doing so, we will also protect our souls. How many children have been led into sin by hearing bad companions using impure language, vaunting in front of them sins of all kinds, or being the cause of some doubt about their family or about the Faith? As for our sense of touch, we must mortify it firmly and constantly. If not, we will quickly be led into sin: maintaining a dignified posture in all circumstances, always dressing in a dignified manner, eating everything served to us, being brief and modest in the care of our bodies, and fleeing idleness.

Finally, it is a real challenge to mortify our imagination, which is easily given to vanity, impurity, and rash judgment. The remedy is to be always occupied.

In order for the Christian virtues to develop, other renouncements and efforts are praiseworthy. In the first place, we must practice a certain poverty in our enjoyment of comfort and material goods. We will come back to this later. Materialism is fundamentally contrary to hope and charity, and, therefore, we must not be surprised that it quite ruins family life.

In the second place, devotion to the family is essential. Examples include the father's coming home from work on time regularly, or all the children's willing and active participation in the regular chores of family life or in the upkeep of the home and property. The husband could, according to his availability, help with the children's homework, attend to odd jobs that need attention around the house, or take care of yard work or the garden, for example. The children should also have assigned chores and responsibilities. Each will love to dedicate himself, not fearing the effort required or the sacrifice of his ease or "comfort zone."

Penance and voluntary sacrifice could also be practiced to touch the Heart of God and to obtain a grace. Intentions are endless: unemployment of the father, illness of the mother, a misunderstanding with one's mother- or father-in-law, a difficult child, conversion of someone, to obtain wisdom for an important decision, financial concerns, etc.

A penance undertaken by the whole family (especially if it lasts for three days), or a novena, will certainly touch the Heart of God. It would be best, in such a case, to choose something within the reach of all, which will not harm anyone's health, and which will not be a burden for some. All should submit to it with a good heart, in a family spirit, and mutually encourage each other.

Each family member could choose his own penance: a decade of the rosary with one's arms in the form of a cross, giving up dessert at lunch, starting with something that is difficult or unpleasant in one's work, etc.

The Love of God and Piety

Religion is often presented as a list of duties or of precepts. We must rise above such a notion. We must discover and live by the love of God. The setting of the family is ideal for such a task because one normally finds emotional love there (feelings) and actual love (proven by acts).

In concrete terms, we see the love of the father and of the mother for the children, and this helps us to envision God the Father and the love of the most holy Virgin for us. St. Therese of the Child Jesus, for example, owed so much to her earthly father, who gave her a good idea of her heavenly Father and of the attitude we should have towards Him.

Let us realize that if the family is penetrated by a true love of God, Christian life will be easy. In fact, the *Imitation of Christ* tells us:

> Love is an excellent thing, a great good indeed, which alone maketh light all that is burdensome and equally bears all that is unequal. For it carries a burden without being burdened and makes all that is bitter sweet and savory. The love of Jesus is noble and generous; it spurs us on to do great things and excites us to desire always that which is most perfect. Love will tend upwards and is not to be detained by things beneath. Love will be at liberty and free from all worldly affections, lest it suffer itself to be entangled with any temporal interest or cast down by losses . . . . The lover flies, runs and rejoices, he is free and not held . . . . Love feels no burden, values no labors, would willingly do more than it can; complains not of impossibility, because it conceives that it may and can do all things.[15]

As St. Francis de Sales so well explained, our love for God must be effective (practical and with all our will) and affective (applying all our heart and gentleness). By this profound charity, God is not simply an idea, a doctrine, but a Person with whom we have a friendship.

This love of each Divine Person facilitates our habitual thought of Their presence and inclines us to have recourse to Them and to seek to please Them in all things, and makes us determined to defend Their honor and the truth. This charity makes it easy to accomplish our duty of state, to wage our spiritual combat, and to support the trials we meet with in life.

This love which binds us with all our being to Our Lord explains our fidelity throughout the crisis in the Church and in society, fidelity without bitterness and without severe judgment on the poor sinners who surround us. By this growing charity, Our Lord becomes all for us, which is why filial fear, the fear of offending God, our Father, drives sin away from us. This is why the desire to advance in virtue abides with us and always inclines us towards spiritual projects.

---

[15] *Imitation of Christ*, Book IV, Ch. 5.

This love of God eliminates in us all that is lacking in charity—criticism, malicious gossip, rash judgments, etc. We need to bear in mind that all these sins deeply wound the Sacred Heart of Our Lord. The reason is that, on the one hand, our tongue is the throne upon which He deigns to descend. On the other hand, those we slander are children of God, and in wounding them, we wound also the Heart of their Father in heaven.

This effective and affective love is, therefore, of the utmost importance, and it must be developed in the heart of the family. The parents are the ones who teach this love because they themselves love and know the joys and fruits of love. They see also the sufferings that occur due to selfishness, which is the disordered love of oneself.

How can we acquire this love which must be the guiding light of our whole lives? It is necessary, firstly, to desire and ask for it ardently. It could be the object of a family novena from time to time. Above all, each should ask for this grace insistently at the time of his First Communion.

We should love to dwell upon all the manifestations of the love of the good God for us, in creation as in the work of Redemption, in joys and in sorrows. As St. Ignatius says, we must consider with great affection all that God our Lord has done for us and how much He desires to give Himself to us. This consideration of the goodness and love of God for us will open hearts and bind them to Him and incline us always to thank Him and give ourselves to Him with joy. The example of the lives of the saints, these friends of God, will carry us along in this path of love of God above all things.

Acts of generosity, freely made for God, will bind us equally to Him: such as holy hours during the night, pilgrimages, etc.

We should love to recite frequent ejaculatory prayers during the day to nourish this flame, so that our spirit and our heart remain penetrated with the presence of God, the joy of knowing the will of God and practicing it. (The practice of the Nine Hours of the Sacred Heart is recommended).

Finally, we must watch that the prayers said in common are said with respect and piety, and that the family solemnizes religious feasts as well as devotions associated with certain months (the Blessed Mother in May, St. Joseph in March, the Sacred Heart in June, etc.). It would be ideal to have a designated area where the statues which surround the crucifix are honored by candles or flowers.

Let us institute, also, a healthy emulation, or competition, in the family for progress in virtue out of love of God. Between the spouses, there is the "duty to sit down," or the duty to find time to talk to each other, to communicate and form their thoughts, ideas, and plans in a calm manner, in order to strengthen their relationship. The time spent with the children can be more informal. In the midst of a private conversation, they might reveal the efforts accomplished and suggest others, for the love of God, giving both natural and supernatural advice. The important thing is for there to be a desire in the soul of the child to become better for the love of God.

The Love of Our Neighbor

In times past, in Christian families, parents impressed upon the hearts of their children such a horror of lying and of stealing that the children remembered the lesson to the day they died. Sins against fraternal charity are even more serious! This is why we must have the same solicitude for correcting these faults and for inculcating the esteem and love of fraternal charity.

Our Lord made it a specific commandment and a mark of His disciples: "Love one another as I have loved you; this is My commandment" (Jn. 15:12), and "By this shall all men know that you are My disciples, if you have love one for another" (Jn. 13:35). This is also the object of the last petition of Jesus' Farewell, or High-Priestly, Prayer: "That they all may be one, as Thou, Father, in Me, and I in Thee; that they also may be one in Us: that the world may believe that Thou hast sent Me" (Jn. 17:21).

Our Lord leaves us this example of charity in the last moments of His life when He washes the feet of His disciples without neglecting Judas the traitor, and when, on the Cross, He pardons His executioners and His enemies, who are far from regretting their actions.

The Divine Master, in addition, further considers the sins done to others as done to Him: "Amen I say to you, as long as you did it to one of these My least brethren, you did it to Me" (Mt. 25:40).

Finally, He manifested the gravity of sins committed against fraternal charity. They close for us access to mercy. "But if you will not forgive men, neither will your Father forgive you your offenses" (Mt. 6:15).

Above all, Jesus does not want us to approach the altar laden with such sins: "If therefore thou offer thy gift at the altar, and there thou remember that thy brother hath anything against thee, leave there thy offering before the altar and go first to be reconciled to thy brother: and then coming thou shalt offer thy gift" (Mt. 5:25).

St. Paul tells us in his turn: "Charity is patient, is kind, beareth all things, believeth all things, hopeth all things, endureth all things" (I Cor. 13:4-7). The Christian family must nourish such an esteem for this virtue that nothing is tolerated in words or actions that can offend against it. On the contrary, all should be done to develop it in all gatherings of family and friends.

Fraternal charity is a supernatural virtue which inclines us to do good to our neighbor out of love of God. As God does good to us, in order to imitate Him, we must do good to our neighbor, inhabited by and moved by the same divine charity, the Holy Ghost.

We now come to some practical aspects of this virtue. The catechism speaks of seven corporal and seven spiritual works of mercy, since our neighbor is composed of body and soul. Let us give some examples which very much concern both family life and how God desires us to act towards our neighbor: "Therefore, while we have time, let us do good to all men, but especially to those who are of the household of the Faith" (Gal. 6:10).

In view of the Mystical Body, let us remember to *visit the sick*. It may happen that one of the spouses or children will have bad health for a certain period of time. Because of that, the other family members will strive to relieve him without indicating that the patient is a burden, but rather accepting in a Christian manner this trial and the resulting consequences. The times of pregnancy and following childbirth are times of fatigue for the mother, for a shorter or longer length of time. All family members should know how to help her with her duties. Throughout it all, let us think of Simon of Cyrene or of St. Veronica, who had the grace to relieve Our Lord on the Way of the Cross.

Concerning the soul of our neighbor, I will dwell an instant on each of the seven manifestations of charity.

The First Spiritual Work of Mercy: To Counsel the Doubtful

First of all, we must counsel the doubtful. Doubt can be a serious calling into question of the Faith or of an aspect of the Faith following a conversation, a lecture, or a period of revolt. Doubt can be accompanied by desolation or can be renewed in the soul of a person who is scrupulous.

Charity and a love of souls incline us to help them to find peace again. In the first place, we need much kindness, and in the second we need much strength.

Let us allow the person to express his doubts in all their ugliness, even if we are shocked by them. The soul is suffering, so let us listen with kindness. Then with strength and firmness, let us demand that he leave all that aside without changing his Christian habits. Remind him that it is impossible to resolve a problem whilst in trouble and agitation of soul.

Finally, when peace has been restored, let us examine the causes. Men and demons have the spirit of rebellion. Nothing in their suggestions can help us to know the truth and to practice it well. Their fruits are obvious because a bad tree does not bring forth good fruit. The one in doubt must not heed their evil suggestions and logic, and he must have sound come-backs.

The Second Spiritual Work of Mercy: To Instruct the Ignorant

It is the role of parents to instruct their children in the basics of the catechism, but even more so to form them to defend themselves against modern errors. To transmit the flame of truth is a beautiful task. We must not be afraid to give it the time needed. Of course, it requires serious formation on the part of the parents.

The couple will love to explain the catechism of Christian doctrine together. Each member of the family must be capable afterwards of teaching the people whom Providence puts in his path.

The drama of many of our contemporaries arises from their ignorance of their religion. The Christian soul must have the desire to spread the light of the truth amongst the ignorant with generosity, as the sower in the Gospel who did not stop at hypotheses or theories.

The Third Spiritual Work of Mercy: To Admonish the Sinner, or Fraternal Correction

This expression evokes punishment or chastisement, and this is an error. Fraternal correction arises from a love of souls and consists in discreetly correcting the sinner so he can amend his life. For the child, the correction could be followed with punishment if necessary.

Today, with much laxity and selfishness, we tend to criticize after the fact! This is not a Christian approach. St. Francis Borgia said: "If you were to wear your clothes inside out or if your face were dirty, would it not be true that someone who would make you aware of it would be showing you charity and that you would thank him for saying so. You would not esteem someone who, to the contrary, having seen the problem, said nothing to you about it. We must, with much greater reason, have the same feelings regarding the faults and imperfections which wound the soul."

It is so important for a soul of good will that aspires to perfection to know its imperfections! It is good for others to tell us of them often enough because we fall quickly back into our base inclinations. Of course, there is a manner of saying it, which must be encouraging and non-wounding, not humiliating. And then, it is necessary to choose the favorable moment when you know that the other is well-disposed.

For children who are in their formative years, fraternal correction will be more frequent. Between spouses, if it is practiced from time to time, it should be done with tact and in private. It will then be most effective, since it may cause a certain suffering or pain.

The Fourth Spiritual Work of Mercy: To Comfort the Sorrowful

Sometimes, it is a matter of moral pains that cause sorrow—for example, failing a test in school, losing a job or a loved one, suffering from a long period of desolation, or from temptations, or the shame of remembering one's sins or errors.

Suffering of the heart can be quite terrible, and it is necessary to exercise much tact and kindness in view of the one who is suffering. In general, one will show much attention to this person, and one will add supernatural arguments to help him pull through his difficulties.

Fifth Spiritual Work of Mercy: To Pardon Offenses

Alas! In families and among families, grudges can be quite tenacious! They must absolutely be cured. Let us not hide behind "good excuses." We must always pardon from the bottom of our hearts, to the extent that we greet everyone and are ready to do good to our enemies if the circumstances present themselves.

We must "overcome evil with good." It is the mystery of the Cross in our relations with others. We cannot be Christian and shirk this obligation. Our Lord tells us: "Love your enemies; do good to them that hate you, and pray for them that persecute and calumniate you: That you may be the children of your Father who is in heaven, who maketh His sun to rise upon the good and the bad and raineth upon the just and the unjust" (Mt. 5:44).

We also know the sentence of the Divine Judge: "But if you will not forgive men, neither will your Father forgive you your offenses" (Mt. 6:15). "Thou wicked servant, I forgave thee all the debt because thou besoughtest me: Shouldst thou not then have had compassion of thy fellow servant, even as I had compassion on thee? And his lord being angry, delivered him to the torturers until he paid all the debt. So also shall My heavenly Father do to you, if you forgive not everyone his brother from your hearts" (Mt. 18:32-35).

Such hard feelings can come from some wound of self-love on the part of one of the spouses: an exaggerated reproach, even if justified; calumnies that have been overheard. Among the children this feeling can be found towards the parents after a correction, or towards their siblings or friends, but it is normally not lasting. On the other hand, among adults, these hard feelings can be tenacious, with an evident lack of charity following upon an injustice, a hurtful word, or even after exaggerated complaints of "victim" by one's neighbor. Sometimes among family members, certain members come to ignore others intentionally and no longer keep in contact with their aged parents or with their brothers and sisters! How are these people part of the family of Our Lord? What an illusion! "If any man say: I love God, and hateth his brother; he is a liar. For he that loveth not his brother whom he seeth, how can he love God whom he seeth not? And this commandment we have from God, that he who loveth God love also his brother" (I Jn. 2:20-21).

To pardon the offenses of our neighbor is to have a normal relationship with him, neither revealing his faults—without grave reason—nor seeking revenge, and being disposed to do him good.

Let us watch out that this Christian attitude reign in our hearts and in our homes! We must have big enough hearts to rise above all these wounds of self-love which offend God and divide souls.

The Sixth Spiritual Work of Mercy: To Bear Wrongs Patiently

Everyone agrees that it is oppressive to live in an atmosphere of screaming, complaining, fits of rage, nervousness and irritation, and of anger. All the members of the family must aspire to a climate of peace. This is why each must exercise patience in the face of set-backs. St. Paul, in his hymn of charity, reveals the first proof of it: "Charity is patient" (I Cor. 13:4). Elsewhere, he places it next to this theological virtue: "And the Lord direct your hearts, in the charity of God and the patience of Christ" (II Thess. 3:5).

We must exercise this patience when faced with any contradiction: "Be patient in suffering" (Rom. 12:12). "Knowing that the trying of your faith worketh patience" (Jas. 1:3). "Reprove, entreat, rebuke in all patience" (II Tim. 4:2). "Put ye on, therefore . . . the bowels of mercy, benignity, humility, modesty, and patience" (Col. 3:12). "Be patient towards all men" (I Thess. 5:14).

Patience is a virtue which moderates the sadness or anger one experiences when faced with evil or confronted by a contradiction. This is why we must be patient with ourselves, with others, and in the trials of life.

Patient with ourselves. We can become impatient because we do not succeed at work or in some project we are trying to accomplish, or due to a fall into temptation, or because we perceive our weakness. Arising from these circumstances, the least word can ignite us, and a bad mood can be read on our faces.

Patient with our neighbor. He has his queer habits, his habitual faults, his lack of education, his negligences, his pace. He can also offend us by his injustices and hurtful words, his fixed opinions, his independence, and his limits. Among these, there are things which are tiresome because they occur so frequently, others which irritate us immediately or which we do not tolerate. Such are the fits of anger, hurtful words, excessive corrections, sulking, and coldness. We forget too often that we have our faults as well, and our shortcomings which try the patience of our neighbor. Also, St. Paul tells us: "Be careful to keep the unity of the spirit in the bond of peace" (Eph. 4:3).

Patient in all circumstances. These include our failures, maladies, setbacks, and anything that goes against our will. In order to maintain interior and exterior peace, each must learn to dominate his passion of sadness or of anger. First of all, it is helpful to meditate on the patience of Our Lord in the Gospel, which He exercised and endured even though He is all-powerful. One word in His Passion summarizes it all: "But Jesus held His peace" (Mt. 26:63). Further, during His public ministry, one sees His patience towards the Pharisees, the crowd who annoys Him, and with the slowness of the disciples in understanding His doctrine. Let us ask Him for a participation in His virtue of patience. Let us also learn to be realistic. We cannot change others, ourselves, or circumstances in an instant. Let us anticipate and accept in advance that which will contradict us so that we might immediately pronounce a *"Fiat"* when these things occur.

Let us be demanding in certain important domains (as in obedience, order, keeping a schedule, respect), and patient in the rest.

It is clear that patience could be a weakness, and therefore a fault, if there were an urgent duty to admonish someone. In that case, such an admonition must be given, not when swayed by anger, but when moved by sound reason, that is to say, with a calm firmness.

The Seventh Spiritual Work of Mercy: To Pray for the Living and the Dead

It is a great act of charity to pray for those around us, for the authorities, and for the departed. A habit of frequently recalling to prayer all our intentions must instill itself in each family.

God wishes to give us much, but only by the means of prayer, prayer both confident and persevering.

The object of our prayer may be thanksgiving, asking pardon of our sins, or asking for graces. In our intentions, let us not forget religious and civil authorities, the dead, the conversion of sinners, the members of our family, those who are suffering, and the souls in purgatory. These prayers could be said in common, specifying the intentions, whether by a decade of the rosary, by a novena, or as part of a confraternity. Let us believe in the power of grace and therefore in the necessity of prayer, and let us know how to say thank you.

Rather than complaining, criticizing, or becoming discouraged, let us have recourse to prayer in common which is so powerful over the Heart of God. Prayer helps us to cast a glance upon our needs and the miseries of men in order to obtain Divine assistance. It is a great act of charity which draws us out of our small personal interests.

Obedience

This is a virtue which we must esteem, love, and make loved. Firstly, it is one of the characteristic virtues of Our Lord. His whole life was one of obedience. He obeyed His parents during His childhood, "He was subject to them" (Lk. 2:51). During His ministry, He obeyed His Father when He had no human authority over Him. "My meat is to do the will of Him who sent Me" (Jn. 4:34). During His Passion, His focus was still on the will of His Father and of the legal authorities: "Father, . . . not My will, but Thine be done" (Lk. 22:42).

"Thou shouldst not have any power against Me, unless it were given thee from above" (Jn. 19:11).

"And whereas indeed He was the Son of God, He learned obedience by the things which He suffered" (Heb. 5:8).

He continues this perfect obedience through the sacraments. Regardless of the priest, his dispositions, the reason for which he confers the sacraments, Christ obeys him. What an abasement is this continual dependence! What an example for us!

Let us see now how the practice of this virtue is necessary for our sanctification.

To obey the legitimate orders of our superiors is to obey God, even if the person has obvious faults or if what he asks of us is not the best thing to do in our opinion. It is necessary to underline this aspect of obedience and try to make it a constant intention: "I obey; I do what is given me to do, because it is God who asks it of me by my husband or my parents."

All spiritual authors note the importance of this virtue and of this intention. Certainly, obedience is difficult for us because it immolates our own will, our independence, but it is a sacrifice sovereignly agreeable to God! What rapid spiritual progress we will make if we exercise the practice of the virtue of obedience!

To accomplish a difficult work by our own will does not at all have the same value as doing a work out of obedience. We must be convinced of this! Children must be well-permeated with this doctrine. We should desire to have to obey all day long rather than command, since by doing so we will be sure of always doing the holy will of God, and therefore grow in His love.

St. Alphonsus Liguori said, "All perfection consists in the love of our infinitely lovable God. Therefore, all the perfection of Divine love consists in the union of our will with that of God. Of course, one is never allowed to commit a fault or a sin out of obedience, or to put his faith or another virtue in danger. In this case, the authority steps beyond the realm of his authority," and it is false obedience to obey such a command.

Finally, obedience allows for the unification of the family. God has willed that, in the womb of the family, authority be centered in the father. To oppose this plan is to oppose unity and is to be an artisan of division. In commanding, the authority figure must seek the will of God by the virtue of prudence. If not, he departs from his sanctification and assumes before God the consequences of the laxity of the exercise of his authority.

The obedience of children towards their parents, under the authority of the father, is not the same obedience that a wife owes her husband. The first is concerned with the formation of virtue in the children, the second with the unity of the family, and indirectly with the good of the home as a whole.

In practice, the use of authority must facilitate the exercise of obedience in demanding little. What is demanded should be in obvious matters. Any order must be clear, precise, and able to be accomplished with little effort. Obeying orders is most often a chance to acquire a quite fragile virtue (obedience) and, of course, to uproot any fault already present.

The authority figure could give explanations of his order so as to help form good judgment, but without forgetting the form of obedience, which is to submit, not because one understands perfectly, but because one wants to accomplish the will of God in all things.

On the other hand, he who obeys will learn to do so promptly and joyfully in order not to render the exercise of authority difficult. There is nothing more painful for a superior than always to hear complaints and objections when he asks something that is just or when he makes a justified remark.

Let us strive to facilitate the exercise of authority among our superiors!

Prudence

This is the main virtue required of one in authority, but it is also the virtue of all Christians who must make decisions throughout life. It is important, for the formation of children, to show them all the facets of the virtue of prudence and to help them to exercise it.

St. Thomas Aquinas summarizes the virtue of prudence in three actions: deliberation, judgment, and commanding. As soon as one of these parts is missing, we become imprudent and fall into the errors of precipitation, or hastiness, rashness, not seeking counsel, indecision, and failure to act at all.

Deliberation

Deliberation is a matter of reflecting and seeking all the advantages in favor of a given decision and then all the inconveniences attendant upon it—the "pros and cons."

Experience teaches us to consider the evolution or development of the advantages and disadvantages likely to result from a decision in one, five, and ten years and their influence over time on the members of the family. As God sees past, present, and future in one instant, so it follows that the authority figure in the family, His representative, must imitate His "forethought" by the virtue of prudence when making decisions, considering the future consequences of his decision.

It is imperative for the one in authority to be completely aware of all that is going on in his family, as work proceeds, in order to grasp the important aspects of problems that arise.

This is the time to take counsel. In the home, it will be the wife who will be the judicious counselor. Her delicate psychology makes her perceive the probable consequences of such and such a decision.

Furthermore, she can suggest other solutions. If the problem is sizable, one could consult other competent people—teachers, a priest, one's parents, or a family friend.

Judgment

Judgment is a matter of finding the best solution for the good of souls and the glory of God. At this step, it is really necessary, if the matter at hand is important, to take a decision in prayer or after receiving the graces of the Mass. The one with authority is the only one this time who is responsible. He must then assume the consequences following upon his decision.

Commanding

It is necessary to give orders and to divide up and assign tasks in order to arrive at the realization of a decision. The authority figure delegates jobs to competent people and then finds out if what he has directed has been carried out and if there were difficulties encountered.

In making major decisions for the family, one must exercise the virtue of prudence when, for example, considering changing one's profession, the family dwelling, making a large purchase, or when choosing family friends or friends for the children. Prudence also must guide us when we are determining visits or outings with members of the couple's families in delicate cases, when deciding about the education of each child, or when giving advice to children considering marriage.

In ordinary cases and those of less importance, these decisions can be made more rapidly, not forgetting the stages of the virtue of prudence.

We must, with St. Thomas, join forethought to the virtue of prudence. Very often, forethought is needed for financial questions. It is necessary, for example, to save money and to ensure that the paying off of the mortgage does not disturb the family or the ability to pay tuition for a good education for the children. Prudence also comes into play in the children's upbringing (for example, this personality defect, what risk will it present in ten years?), in planning a vacation (what will be done on Sunday?).

To live by caprice, day by day, with no planning for the near or far future, is exhausting for those around us who need security and organization.

Fostering a Spirit of Poverty

Our Lord willed to be born into a poor family, to be surrounded by poor disciples, and to make this virtue the first of the Beatitudes: "Blessed are the poor in spirit." This choice is an example for us. Our Lord's exercise of this virtue is a prime example for us, and it, above all, must not be neglected! Only having a detachment from the goods of this world can make us appreciate and desire true riches, which are those of the heart and of the soul.

In a poor family, one turns towards the essential things, and therefore one has time to pray, to visit with each other, and, having little or nothing, to do things together. Terrestrial goods do not, then, become objects of disordered affection or of covetousness.

The education of children obliges us to make real financial sacrifices. It is a grace for the whole family! Neither comfort, nor outings, nor expensive sports, nor even being able to satisfy our desires are the important thing. The important possessions are strong virtue, union of hearts, and solid piety.

Let us remember that Cardinal Pie said already in his time, "Materialism engenders sensuality and selfishness." As soon as there is a lot of money in the house, it is not rare to see that each spouse becomes more and more occupied with his own interests and pleasures, and hence the relationship becomes very fragile. As for the children, they become demanding, selfish, and independent. They also tend to lack courage.

In putting the virtue of poverty into practice, let us say that it is normal for children to share a room, for bathrooms to be in common, and for homework and games to take place in a common room where the mother works. Each child's toys should be simple and few. Each child should participate in family chores on a regular basis. It is good for vacations to take place in the country, without too many expenses. It is imperative that the TV, video games, and Internet be banished from the home for the preservation of virtue, especially that of poverty and of purity.

As for clothes, all the members of the family should keep them until they are worn out, regardless of the fashion. Furniture should be of the most simple and solid style, being capable of lasting a lifetime. The decoration of the rooms should also be simple and discreet. Cleanliness and order will then be easier to maintain.

One should not accumulate useless things, but be happy with simple things, even in one's library. Outside of a few basic books (Catholic works, a missal), the other books should pass from hand to hand. Also, objects of piety should be the essentials, always in good taste.

Poverty will not impede making gifts to works of charity, for Masses to be said, or for the poor. This virtue facilitates richness of the heart and generosity.

Poverty can make us pass through difficult moments. It is then that confidence in God and in His providence will take on a whole new dimension. Let us read again the prediction of Our Lord which ends with these words: "Seek ye, therefore, first the kingdom of God and His justice, and all these things will be given you besides" (Mt. 6:24-34).

And then let us love to say again with confidence: "Our Father, who art in heaven, . . . give us this day our daily bread."

Devotion and Exterior Zeal

It is fundamental for the couple to understand that the family is not a smaller society which lives closed in upon itself in order to protect it from the world. We are social beings, and we must live in the world without, however, taking on the spirit of the world. "Love not the world, nor the things that are of the world. If any man love the world, the charity of the Father is not in him" (I Jn 2:14). To be in the world without being of the world is an aspect of our exile in this sinful world. We cannot escape it.

Among the souls who live at the same time as we, there are those whom we can help along the way of their salvation. Our Lord gave us a duty. Just after having enunciated the Beatitudes, which ought to transform our lives, He evokes our mission in the world: "You are the light of the world. A city seated on a mountain cannot be hid. Neither do men light a candle and put it under a bushel, but upon a candlestick, that it may shine to all that are in the house. So let your light shine before men that they may see your good works and glorify your Father who is in heaven" (Mt. 5:14-16).

A united, happy, Christian family that has simple relationships with everyone can very quickly give advice, can sow the word of God, and will be listened to because it is esteemed. Quite often, what first touches people is the good upbringing of children, their politeness, their conversations, and their soundness of mind.

One could propose a novena of prayers on the part of the whole family for a person who is suffering, or offer him a holy picture, or a medal with an assurance of the family's prayers. Sometimes, one could propose the visit of a priest or accompany him to Mass.

This apostolic side of the family uplifts souls and brings them joy. The children learn the habit of zeal, which is a clear manifestation of the love of God. Certainly, the successes of the undertakings today are rare, but is not the most important thing to manifest our supernatural charity?

A right relationship with the world will help us to progress in the spirit of mercy. It is easy, in keeping a certain distance from the world, to judge severely those who surround us, based on their actions and their words. But in approaching their hearts, one can discern good dispositions, unknown sufferings, and invincible ignorance. Then excuses become easy and good influence is possible.

Little by little, one realizes the force of the media with its preconceived ideas and fashionable opinions on souls of good will who would be good Christians in a Catholic society. The gravity of the religious liberty preached by the current authorities appears in all its ugliness.

This state of affairs demonstrates the consequences of the absence of a Christian education and of the absence of grace in one's life. With these sentiments of pity in the face of the poor and miserable of this world, we can better appreciate what we have received and decide to treasure it more. For those who are perceptive and grateful, such a realization will prolong itself into a prayer of thanksgiving, but also of reparation and petition.

Acting thus as a family, we will not let ourselves be contaminated, but will develop in our hearts more and more mercy. All hardness of heart or of bitter zeal will disappear in our souls.

Finally, our devotedness in the world will greatly aid in the formation of maturity in our children. In earlier ages, Christian families would readily visit the sick, the suffering, and the aged. This contact with suffering greatly helps the children to mature and to escape from a life that is too easy and too comfortable.

Children can also show their dedication to the friends of the family on the occasion of maternity, sickness, or a move. Not infrequently, children spontaneously manifest much outward generosity. Parents ought not to be afraid of giving them the opportunity to do so.

For those children who show devotedness in the neighborhood, one of the parents should always be present with the child in order to prevent any possible bad influences.

The priories and the schools are also easy occasions for us to show our dedication. It is with joy that we must give of ourselves to them. It is a matter of avoiding a selfish life which is easy and too comfortable. It is also the chance to give God our time and abilities, recognizing all that He has done for us. We will always be indebted to Him! Let us have a great supernatural spirit which renders things easy and more meritorious: "It is for the good God."

Some Remaining Essential Virtues

I will quickly mention some other virtues which must be cast into the foundation of the family. Not long ago, they were obvious. Today they are less so. This is why I will give some suggestions for each of them.

Respect, Which Excludes Undue Familiarity or Inconsiderateness

Each man, when he speaks with his wife, will do so with respect. Therefore, he should eliminate displeasing vocabulary which is scornful and proud. In his attitude and in his attire, he should watch that he avoid all sloppiness, negligence, and immodesty.

Children should be well-instructed as regards showing respect towards their parents and superiors—the manner of answering them and of speaking to them. For this, they should remember all that they owe them. Children should respect other adults as well, and the elderly. This will be shown in their courteousness and the ease with which they accept advice.

Finally, everyone should be careful to respect and to take care of the objects at his disposal or which he has borrowed (books, games, devices).

Having a Good Outlook, Simple Joy

Nothing is more depressing in a family than the atmosphere of constant criticism, complaining, sulking, coldness, or indifference. Everyone likes to be in a peaceful, joyful, and pleasant home, where everyone is attentive to each other, and where each gives an account of his day, and knows how to have fun.

Of course, this good attitude sometimes requires sacrifices of us for a number of reasons. It is easy to be preoccupied. Someone always has some sort of suffering to deal with. Someone else has been wounded or insulted, and wishes to remain silent because he has a reserved and quiet personality. But let us learn to set aside and overcome all these concerns in order to foster a good family atmosphere.

Having Order in Things and in One's Schedule

Disorder occasions much impatience in family life. It is necessary to do everything to avoid these sins against our neighbor.

It is normal for each member of the family to establish order in his own affairs. It is not the job of the mother to chase after everyone! To achieve order, it is necessary for everyone to develop the habit of putting and keeping things in their place.

Order gives peace and contentment at the glance of an eye. It makes it easy to find things, and keeps one from accumulating unnecessary junk. It also helps to avoid wasting time. Children learn very early the discipline of order, and it will help them all their lives.

To rise on time, to be on time for prayers, for Mass, for meals, and for outings is indispensable for the common good. We must learn not to make others wait. Lack of punctuality is at the root of arguments, hurtful words, coldness, all of which can be avoided if we acquire the habit of what was once called "the courtesy of kings."

Perseverance in All Things

Nothing is more destructive to the intellectual life, the spiritual life, or family and social life, than inconstancy in one's actions and activities. It is explained by laziness or the bad habit of starting too many things at once. It affects one's studies, one's spiritual efforts, one's family projects, and one's apostolate.

We must practice the virtue of perseverance in little things from our childhood. If not, our souls will fall very quickly into caprice and superficiality. Without sacrifice, we cannot acquire this virtue that St. Thomas attaches to the virtue of fortitude. To attain it, it is necessary to be modest in the goals which we make for ourselves and the exterior commitments we take upon ourselves or that we try to control.

Strength of Soul against the Spirit of the World

How many children, from the young to adults, are overcome by the influence of the world! They are lacking solid convictions and the strength of character to assert themselves and to affirm their convictions.

It follows from this distinct character weakness that they easily make concessions to the spirit of the world, and little by little, let themselves be transformed by the world. All the while they falsify their consciences by meaningless expressions like, "We cannot be fanatics," "You've got to be up with the times," etc.

The more contact we have with the world, the more our manner of thinking, of speaking, and of living departs from Christian living as well as from the ideal of sanctification. In the upcoming generation, nothing will remain of the principles they have received if they do not gain this beautiful virtue of strength of soul, which entails learning to overcome human respect.

This is a serious problem of which we must be well aware. If we do not enlist ourselves in this combat against error and the evil means and modes of acting of the modern world, we are lost. Of course, it is a matter of a combat originating and moved by the love of God and the spirit of mercy regarding the poor world which is often the victim of the current liberalism and laxity in the Church and in society.

This combat necessitates the persevering study of the evil from which the world suffers in the light of Catholic doctrine. It is undertaken by keeping abreast of this evil and by little controlled conflicts with it; confronting the world, while being sustained and supported by people with solid formations.

May Catholic Spouses Consider Separation?

This question presents itself, alas, to certain people when serious difficulties arise in the home.

Let us give a few examples: the personalities of the spouses are so different that they argue constantly; one of the spouses launches a religious persecution against the other; one is violent, is an alcoholic, is impure; there is a real conflict in the upbringing and education of the children, in the exercise of authority; one of the spouses is always on the back of the other; the husband does not fulfill his duties and does not hold down a job, or he has a tyrannical authority; or the wife keeps absolutely no schedule, allows disorder to reign, or wants to boss everyone around.

It is clear that sometimes common life resembles an oppressive burden and seems beyond one's ability to endure. So you think of giving up and separating. The world proposes divorce in order to remake one's life in better conditions, supposedly. The Catholic thinks of a solution which seems to respect his commitment to indissolubility—physical separation.

Let us say right off that to consider this solution or even this possibility, is a trick of the devil. It draws you away from your commitments and distances you from Catholic solutions!

Understand well that your vows taken before the Church also include the obligation of life in common. Therefore, only the Church, after a judgment, can decide to dispense from life in common—for a time or indefinitely—and the spouses remain married before God.

The Church is justly severe with those who take this initiative without serious and urgent reason. The canonist Naz writes: "Even the authors who show themselves the most liberal demand the intervention of the Church, excepting the case of adultery. Even when the motive is certain and urgent, it seems well that the decision be only provisional and the spouse must receive approval from the Ordinary before doing so."

In practice, one must never think this [an anullment] is a possibility, unless a priest who knows you well advises you to consider it seriously in light of the circumstances of your life. Following upon such advice from a priest, one must address himself to the competent authority recommended by said priest who will lodge the inquiry and give its judgment. In order to help you through these difficult moments, it is good always to bear in mind both the serious consequences of separation and Catholic alternatives.

First of all, it is a very bad example given both to Catholics and to people in the world. Any person hearing of it would think he could follow suit and perhaps end up justifying living in sin with someone. It would seem that the sacrament of marriage would be powerless to bind two souls for life, and the temptation would arise to wonder, why bother with marriage in the Church at all?

It is also obvious to everyone that the children will be the greatest victims of this situation. Each of the spouses will have the temptation to show the faults of the other and to spoil the children in order to attach them to himself. Children who are capricious are the obvious fruits of such an arrangement and may perhaps also end up hating their parents, perceiving that they have destroyed their lives.

How many times have I seen children prefer a family atmosphere that is oppressive to one that is rent asunder by a separation! The resulting disequilibrium disrupts their lives, to say the least. In addition, how can these children envision marriage for themselves, not having had an example of stability?

Separation clearly puts the spouses in real danger of an immoral and sinful life. Solitude and continence are also imposed on each. In the world in which we live, such a situation could very quickly become beyond the strength of one or the other to endure. Solicitations are numerous and falls are all the easier and the more frequent when the spiritual life is abandoned and one lives in a state of sadness and failure.

Solitude can also be an occasion to sink into crude habits—alcoholism, general carelessness, addiction to the TV, to the Internet, to Facebook and similar social networking online.

We come now to the Christian solutions to these problems. These solutions are summarized in the mystery of the Cross, in prayer, and in the good will of each one involved.

Let us note, first of all, before arriving at such an extremely tense situation, that there are some signs that should warn us of an impending crisis. Let us learn how to recognize the symptoms and find simple solutions which re-establish confidence and good will on one part or the other. You could organize a week of vacation for an exhausted husband, take more time to communicate and visit with each other, organize more frequent recreation time together, make a retreat away from the home, seek help from a priest, or increase the attention you give your spouse. To fail to make the first conciliatory move is to let the situation deteriorate from day to day, and your children are the first to suffer.

On nearly every retreat that I preach, I am edified by the generosity and supernatural outlook of husbands and wives who live in very difficult situations. In heaven, we shall see the merits of the people who have learned, day after day, to renounce and to overcome themselves. They will have an eternal recompense! In addition, they have clothed their souls in heroic virtue and obtained great graces for their family. In eternity, in view of the beatitude they have obtained by their sacrifices and perseverance, they will say, "If I had to do it all again, I would not hesitate a moment."

The first attitude, the first reaction, to have when common life becomes difficult is to be supernatural and to be realistic. That is to say, to see the magnitude of the difficulties and then to accept them, proposing to fight with the corresponding virtues—strength, patience, humility. St. Ignatius calls this the *"agere contra"* rule—to fight with the virtue opposed to the temptation one is experiencing.

We must accept and offer up these pains, that is to say, to speak to no one about it (other than our confessor, who can help us) and to maintain a good attitude and a smile. Of course, one cannot attain this level without recourse to prayer and frequent reception of the sacraments.

The second attitude consists in assuming that each has a good will. There is always, thus, a chance for the situation to improve. To achieve an improvement, the best thing to do is to consult a priest or a friend of the family. A double-sided question then presents itself to each spouse: "What are the three efforts that I am ready to make to strengthen our family life and get it back on the right track?" and "What are the three essential efforts that I expect from my spouse?" Fortified with these responses, a third party would point out one or two areas for each spouse to try to improve upon until they are corrected and perfected.

The third attitude resides in confident prayer and a common spiritual life. When the reconciliation of personalities is almost impossible, recourse must be had to prayer and the spiritual life. There truly are married couples who have saved their marriages by retreats and honest spiritual effort. Let us believe in the power of grace!

Sometimes, you cannot get beyond the first solution. You have at least to attempt the second, at any rate, ignoring all scornful reproach, as well as the silent treatment. As St. Paul tells us, let us try to overcome evil with good. It is necessary to do everything in order to be found blameless in the eyes of God.

If, unfortunately, separation is forced upon you, carry this cross with resignation and without complaining. Redouble your prayers, maintain your balance by good relationships and healthy distractions, be firm in your schedule, and shun luxury, the Internet, and social networking.

Always be ready to forgive, forget, and begin common life again. Offer up your personal sufferings and those arising from the fact that others are looking down on you, for the salvation of your family.

And keep your hopes up!

To conclude, I would like to give some extracts from the life of St. Rita.[16] Firstly, the author reminds us of the example of St. Monica:

---

[16] Msgr. De Marchi, *Life of St. Rita*.

Married against her inclination to a pleasure-seeking and choleric pagan, and entering into a home where she was greeted by an ill-disposed mother-in-law, Monica took the resolution right away to do everything to please her husband—as long as it was not against the law of God—in order thus to obtain his conversion. If he was in a bad mood, Monica held her tongue. This she did so well that the other women, who were used to being beaten by their husbands, marveled that she never suffered this humiliation. She finally succeeded, by the force of her patience and her prayers, in enrolling Patrick, her husband, among the catechumens, and in preparing him for a good Christian death.

Without doubt, Rita had heard of the mother of St. Augustine. She, then, had a model to imitate in establishing her home. Like St. Monica, she prayed for the conversion of her husband. Like her, also, she bore in silence his fits of anger and his insults, and did all she could to make her home attractive so that he might find there everything to make him happy. I am using few words to describe the situation, but women who have such a husband will know what a bitter trial it is to their patience and how difficult it is to make such a man happy! He flew off the handle for no reason at all, cursing, swearing, insulting, and beating anyone who got in his way, loading his poor wife with insults, who, during his rage, either responded with bitter remarks or a frightened burst of tears.

For Rita's husband, this obnoxious behavior gained him many enemies. Offended at this turn of events, he sought to avenge his anger. Being unable to do so, he brought his troubles home, and his innocent wife bore the brunt of his rage. These were violent and brutal scenes. Spurred on by wine and anger, Paul would lose complete control, beating anyone around him, shouting and cursing in a revolting manner, horrifying poor Rita and causing her to despair. The day was not long in coming when, weary of failing to obtain his desires, Paul vented his anger on Rita, and the blows caused her to weep. One day, she was only saved from death by the providential intervention of her parents.

But how did she come to such faith and charity? Rita remembered the words of Our Lord, "If you have faith like unto a mustard seed, you will say to a mountain, 'Remove and throw yourself into the sea,' and the mountain will obey." Her patience was so heroic that her neighbors called her "the woman devoid of hard-feelings." This marvelous moral strength was proof of her fervent prayer, of her holy communions, and of her favorite meditation, that of the Passion of Our Lord Jesus Christ. In thinking upon the ingratitude shown Him—the insults, the mockeries, and the blows received, innocent though He was—her own cross seemed light in comparison. What caused her pain was to see His pierced Heart and to know that Paul was His enemy and that he would be damned to hell.

In order to obtain his conversion, she joined difficult penances to her prayers. Each year she fasted for three Lents instead of one. Bear in mind that the Lent of her time was quite rigorous to start with—only one small meal allowed in the evening, and nothing other than that. Let us recall this young woman, overwhelmed with work and sorrows, who suffered in complete silence, while blessing God, and we will not be surprised that, little by little, she helped to calm her husband and draw him nearer to God. Insulted without reason, she spoke no word of resentment; beaten, she did not complain, and she was so obedient that she did not even go to church without the permission of her brutal husband. But finally the day arrived when the lamb triumphed over the wolf. Paul began to reflect and to admire the incomparable patience of his victim. He was ashamed. When he felt his anger rising, he left the house until it was defused, and he did not return until he had regained his composure.

The grace of God triumphed in his savage nature, and became to Rita a great consolation when, one day, he threw himself at her feet, truly repentant, and covered her hands with kisses and sobbed, "Forgive me, Rita! I have been unworthy of you, but I promise to change. Your tremendous kindness has saved me and has helped me to understand finally what true life is." He kept his promise.

The Spiritual Life of the Home

Anyone who desires a Christian home which is united and stable, must build it on a rock (Mt. 7:24).

And this rock is God!

The first three commandments, as well as the first three petitions of the Our Father, remind us that God is the foundation of any life of perfection. Without God, we are nothing, and we build on sand. The current situation in the Church clearly manifests this to us.

In practice, we must introduce the Sacred Heart into the hearts of our homes—He is the source of all graces—and the Blessed Virgin, who is the Mother of mercy.

After these devotions, in order to gain graces for each member of the home so as to triumph over their temptations and progress in virtue and in the love of God, there must be prayer in common.

Each needs his time for serious reflection, or taking "time out." This is provided by an annual retreat, a monthly retreat, or by spiritual reading.

The family is not an entity unto itself. It also needs spiritual activities with other families, for example, pilgrimages.

The Enthronement of the Sacred Heart in the Home and the Consecration of the Family to the Immaculate Heart of Mary

The Divine Savior and the Queen of the world love to find homes where they know they are part of the family, where they are at home. Everything there gives them a respite from the world and consoles them in this world: the spirit of piety found there, their mutual respect, their patience in suffering, their zeal for souls, and their devotion.

What an honor for a family to be a refuge for Jesus and Mary in these times of indifference and impiety! But we must be worthy of it.

This must be the objective of a good Christian family! Once done, Jesus and Mary can draw vocations from among the children. By so doing, Jesus and Mary establish a line of spiritual parenthood ever greater with the happy family.

The Enthronement of the Sacred Heart

To all who manifest a true devotion to Him, the Sacred Heart has made promises worthy of His love for us:

> I will give them all the graces necessary for their state of life.
>
> I will grant peace to their family.
>
> I will be their consolation in suffering.
>
> I will bestow abundant blessings on all their undertakings.
>
> Lukewarm souls will become fervent.
>
> Fervent souls will attain great perfection.
>
> I will bless every home where an image of My Heart will be exposed and honored.

For the enthronement, one should ask a priest for advice concerning the preparation and ceremony.

The picture or the statue of the Sacred Heart should be placed in the most worthy room in the house (the living room), which will become the place for family prayers.

It is good to pay particular attention to the beauty of the area reserved for the enthroned image. It is easy to understand that the enthronement of the Sacred Heart is not compatible with the television, which poisons the family with the spirit of the world and ruins the family spirit. The same can be said of the use of the Internet outside of professional uses—such as web-surfing, Facebook, or other social networks. Let us recall the words of Holy Scripture: "Adulterers, know you not that the friendship of this world is the enemy of God? Whosoever therefore will be a friend of this world becometh an enemy of God" (Jas. 4:4).

The anniversary of the enthronement is a good time to renew the enthronement of the Sacred Heart, with or without the presence of a priest. The celebration of this day should be crowned with a holiday-style meal.

Every day, if possible, family prayers should be recited in this place. In addition, in family needs, sufferings, thanksgiving, and important decisions, it is a good idea to reunite the family around the Sacred Heart to confide our intentions to Him.

We should also make it a duty to ask pardon and to repair offenses to God of which we have been a witness. We will love to console the Sacred Heart during a family holy hour. The members of the home will make a point of practicing the First Fridays of the month in a spirit of reparation and of love.

Finally, each should make it a duty to struggle effectively against his habitual fault, especially in the home (since "charity begins at home"), in order to be more worthy of the Sacred Heart.

Consecration to the Immaculate Heart

Pius XII wrote: "In order that favors in greater abundance may flow on all Christians, nay, on the whole human race, from the devotion to the most Sacred Heart of Jesus, let the faithful see to it that to this devotion the Immaculate Heart of the Mother of God is closely joined."[17] And he adds that all families ought to consecrate themselves to the Immaculate Heart of Mary! This act of piety will be a precious help for couples in the practice of their duties of chastity and conjugal fidelity. They will be able to keep the virtue of purity present in the home while raising their children.

Naturally, families place an image of the Immaculate Heart of Mary to the right of her Divine Son. Mary will intercede for each

---

[17] Encyclical *Haurietis Aquas,* §124.

of the happy members of the family. In addition to the rosary, one should solemnize the months of May and October, responding to the demands of Our Lady of Fatima: "On the five First Saturdays of the month, recite often the prayers of the angel, and add to your sacrifices the beautiful prayer, 'O Jesus, it is for love of You, in reparation to the Immaculate Heart of Mary, and for the conversion of sinners.'"

Prayer in Common

The home, as well as all society, created by God, has a duty to render honor to God. This is why the authority figure, the head of the family, organizes prayers in common in the home and leads them as often as he can. Since it is the family that prays as one, there should be a sense of unity in prayer, so the prayers should be in unison.

Respect for God will be manifested by one's posture (kneeling) and recollection. If the children are distracted or are a distraction, one could say prayers with them a little later.

It is important to watch that prayers recited together are not too long or started too late in the evening. Private devotions could be encouraged. Of course, keep in mind the ages of the children when choosing prayers.

Let us not forget that prayer is talking to God and not a recitation. This is why some words about the presence of God, the love of God, and our state of being a child before God are necessary.

Morning Prayers

Morning prayers should be made in two stages: (1) The first set of prayers is said as one gets out of bed, on one's knees. It is the Morning Offering, three Hail Mary's, and ended with, "O my Mother, preserve me from mortal sin during this day." (2) The second set is said kneeling before the Sacred Heart. These morning prayers can be the morning prayers found in the retreat manual, *Christian Warfare*. They can be shortened for young children. These prayers obtain for us the necessary graces to live as a good Christian this day. They give us the chance to renew our resolution to struggle against our main fault (which we will try humbly to discover).

The Angelus

The Angelus should be recited by the whole family, standing, before the three meals of the day. The father should lead if present; if not, the mother. The same should lead the thanksgiving after meals.

During paschal time, the Regina Cæli is recited in place of the Angelus.

When one is invited to a home where prayers are not normally said, it should be explained that one is used to praying before eating. You could also just say your blessing yourself, depending on the circumstances.

The Rosary

Our Lady, Mediatrix of all graces, asks us in each of her apparitions to recite the rosary every day. We cannot shirk this duty.

Let us avoid beginning it too late! It is a good habit to say it before the evening meal. In order to render this family prayer easier and more fruitful, it is good for each to reflect a minute on the virtue he desires to meditate upon in each mystery.

On Sunday, one could recite the rosary before Mass or during a walk together, being careful to stay recollected.

In the months of May and October, it is good to add the litany of the Blessed Virgin. In addition, during the months of March and June, add the litanies of St. Joseph and of the Sacred Heart respectively.

Night Prayers

These prayers are very important. After the strain and worries of the day, we place everything in the hands of God. After all the faults and disorders of the day, everyone asks pardon of God and can rest in peace.

For the little ones, their night prayers consist of an offering of their efforts, of thanksgiving, an examination of conscience, and an act of contrition. The mother gives some suggestions to help them discover their sins of the day.

It is impossible to insist enough on the importance of the examination of conscience. Without this regular and profound practice, even though grave sins are eliminated, one lives a superficial and mediocre existence.

It is good to include in it the examination of piety, fraternal charity, the spirit of sacrifice, justice, obedience, humility, promptness in doing one's duty, zeal for souls, purity of intention in our actions, patience, pardoning offenses—distinguishing among faults of thought, word, action, and omission.

For the older ones, evening prayers are said with the parents, using the retreat manual or *Christian Warfare*. For the examination of conscience, simply allow a sufficient moment of silence, offering obvious suggestions. This prayer is directed by the head of the family when he is there, and is ended by an Act of Contrition and three Hail Marys to ask for the grace of purity.

Normally, night prayers are said before putting the little ones to bed. It is good to recite them before the children are too tired and lose their attention. The parents could make a short visit to each child as he is tucked in. It could be a chance to allow him to confide in the parent, but it should not be too drawn out.

Important Points

The Annual Retreat

Priests and religious who live relatively retired from the world make a retreat once a year. How much more necessary is it for married couples who live in the world! who are continually in contact with the spirit of the world!

The Spiritual Exercises of St. Ignatius enable us to find again our purity of heart and to strengthen our souls to better fulfill our duties. Regular attendance at retreats has become a necessity in the modern world. Let us cite a couple of authorities in the Church who encourage it: "St. Ignatius learned from the Mother of God how to direct the combats of Our Lord. . . . He received the rules so perfectly that the soldiers of Jesus Christ must use them" (Pope Pius XI, *Mens Nostra*, 1929). "The benefits of the Spiritual Exercises are such for the salvation of souls and their progress in the Christian life that the sovereign pontiffs have not ceased to praise and encourage the clergy and faithful to make them periodically" (Archbishop Lefebvre, October 1976).

For married couples, the best course of action is to co-ordinate their retreats in the same month in order to harmonize and to support each other in their resolutions. Retreats from the home are an effective complement to home life. It is good to attend them as regularly as one's confessor advises.

Spiritual Reading

We live in a world where there is hardly a conversation that is good for our souls. This is why there is a grave need to nourish our minds and hearts regularly by spiritual reading which will maintain in us the ideal of the Christian life.

Just as we need to be spurred on by the good example we see in others, so also do we need to read the lives and writings of the saints. These books can be read and re-read, as we will always find in them material for our edification. All the same, reading a multitude of authors can cause dissipation or curiosity of spirit.

This reading can easily be done in the evening with the family after the dishes. It allows for an edifying sharing of ideas between the spouses.

Here are a few basic books which every family should have and read:

- *The Four Gospels in One* by Weber
- *The Imitation of Christ* by Thomas à Kempis

- *Introduction to the Devout Life* by St. Francis de Sales
- *The Way of Perfection* by St. Teresa of Avila
- *A Treatise on Prayer, The Instruments of Perfection*, and *The Twelve Degrees of Humility* by Dom Jean de Monleon
- *Christ, the Life of the Soul* by Abbot Marmion
- *The Soul of the Apostolate* by Dom Chautard
- *Holy Abandonment* by Dom Lehodey
- *Spiritual Combat* by Fr. Scupoli
- The Works of St. Louis de Montfort
- The Works of St. Alphonsus Liguori
- *Commentary on the Old Testament* by Dom de Monleon
- Lives of the Saints
- Fr. Alain Delagneau's bulletin, *Marchons Droit*
- *The Family Catechism* by Fr. Emmanuel
- *The Catechism of Marriage* by Fr. Noel Barbara
- Works on Catholic Education, from *Marchons Droit*
- *An Explanation of the Mass* by Fr. Cochen
- *The Mass of All Time* by Archbishop Lefebvre

Monthly Recollection

It can be said of Christian marriage that two beings unite their destinies before God, in the eyes of the Church, in order to progress together in the path of virtue and of sanctity. Marriage is the creation of a small society of common life where the spouses must support each other in order to advance, one by the other and with the other, in the way of perfection. The main goal is not, therefore, to amass earthly goods, to have every comfort known to man, or always to enjoy the sweet life, but to sanctify oneself well and beautifully in and by family life.

In addition, the real questions that one must ask oneself are these: Today, after three or five years of marriage, or more, are we both more virtuous and more united than on the day of our marriage? Have we each grown by the circumstances of common life to know how to educate and raise our children; to understand the differences between our characters; to perceive the different way we see things; to embrace the duties of state we each have; to accept our trials; to sanctify the relationships we have with our family members and our friends; to share our decisions and common duties? In fact, in order that all the circumstances of common life become effective means of perfection for both spouses, they must know how to manage them, how to tackle them together.

It is clear that in the beginning of marriage, the spouses find time to talk to each other, to confide in each other with a certain depth, and when needed, to smooth things over, or settle each other down. Their love is still in its first fervor, is zealous, full of concern for the other and of self-abnegation.

With the passage of time, children come along, duties of state become exhausting, and different occupations and cares of the family and of the home become absorbing. The couple is less and less alone, and when they are, they prefer a climate of rest and of tenderness rather than taking time to reflect on home issues, to examine the way they need to avoid the slackening off which draws nature down, and the way to grow in virtue.

After the honeymoon is over, the faults of each appear. One accepts one's own faults, unless the other points them out. Sometimes, there are even shows of strength, each wanting to impose his own will and not wanting to consider the complaints of the other. Thus, they understand each other less and less, and finally arrive at a certain resignation (or hopelessness), a *modus vivendi*, a way of getting along.

Finally, one or the other loses his zeal for sanctity, no longer having plans for advancing in virtue or for helping the other in his or her sanctification.

In order to avoid falling into this lukewarmness, it is indispensable to organize, after annual retreats, a practice that bears good fruit, which is called

"THE DUTY TO SIT DOWN"

What is it all about?

It is to stop, once a month, together, beneath the gaze of God in order to evaluate and enliven their mutual sanctification. Let us observe the contents of this program.

To Stop

This means to isolate oneself so as to be able to concentrate easily and peacefully on the essential. In practice, it means the setting aside of all that could interrupt this important conversation—the children should be in bed or with friends, the telephone needs to be off the hook.

A relaxed atmosphere is also important to facilitate this heart to heart. You could begin with some relaxation together, for example, a game, some sort of pleasant manual labor, or a nature walk. Plan enough time so that your tête-à-tête does not extend too late in the evening—around an hour or two is ideal.

Once a Month

A regular schedule is necessary. Experience shows that for there to be real continuity and for it not to be too burdensome, it is good to space these "meetings" out by a month. Thus, the time in between allows enough space for there to be improvement, but not too much time for a relapse.

A month seems ideal. The date and the hour must be fixed in order not to be tempted to procrastinate. For example, you could plan for the first Sunday of the month from three to five p.m., or from eight to ten p.m.

Together

This implies that there be an equal participation on the part of the spouses.

It should not be just one who analyzes and dissects the actions and deeds of the other while trying to justify oneself! No, it should not be an accusation, nor a settling of scores, nor a moral lesson! Rather, each opens his heart, that is to say, explains with delicateness and humility what has happened during the month concerning the family.

Beneath the Eyes of God

In the end, there should be an examination of conscience on both sides regarding their contribution to the home—not a personal examination—and a taking of practical resolutions to sanctify, to heal, to rejuvenate, and to console the home. After this meeting, the two spouses should feel full of zeal, as though Our Lord had visited them.

It is essential to believe that this sort of meeting is feasible and workable. Here are two children of God who, beneath the eyes of God who probes their hearts, take stock of their lives. This colloquy is made, then, with three people. It is obvious that when the goal is to help the couple draw nearer to each other, they ought to put God in the picture as a focal point, as a destination.

It is necessary, then, to begin each of these meetings with some prayers—the Veni Creator or the Our Father, and not to hesitate in their midst to renew these prayers.

The presence of God helps each one to remain humble, merciful, and charitable. They, therefore, are precious. Take these words more and more to heart: "When two . . . are gathered in My name, I am there in the midst of them" (Mt. 18:20).

What a grace! What an encouragement!

Taking Stock

To get started, one could quickly review the little grievances or animosities which one has had against the other. You almost have to do this by making fun of yourself so the other will retain the essence of the point made and leave aside what is in his imagination and which is a matter of self-love. This must be delicately done so that the spouse does not throw up his defenses.

One word of apology will encourage the offended one to mercy and to complete pardon. Nothing is worse than buried resentments which are badly digested. The abscess must be lanced before it can heal. It is not always easy, but an act of humility attracts graces of peace.

Afterwards, one can proceed to more important questions:

God—personal and familial piety, edifying considerations of what God is expecting of you.

The children—take a look at each one and consider his piety, virtues, faults, school work, abilities, the dangers confronting him, the school.

Social life—the family, colleagues, the neighbors, friends, get-togethers with other families.

The married couple itself—the role of each, the complementarity of education, suggestions concerning organization, the practice of virtue.

Personal life—inspection of each concerning the regularity of his life, without touching the realm of conscience. However, one's spouse is often the best judge in evaluating one's struggle against one's predominant fault.

Conclude with taking practical and simple common resolutions.

Inspiring in Each Other the Desire for Mutual Sanctification

The whole discussion will be dominated by this motive of charity. It is a matter of helping the other to become better and agreeing to be helped to advance in virtue. The children will be the primary beneficiaries!

The topics covered must be encouraging, give a desire to progress for the love of God and of one's spouse.

The meeting is concluded with a prayer for each other in order to profit from these reflections.

Some might object: this style of meeting seems artificial. It would be better to explain oneself and to consult each other as work proceeds.

To that I respond: Do not oppose what is a complement to what you are trying to accomplish! The annual retreat does not replace the monthly recollection. By the same token, daily conversations do not replace "the duty to sit down!"

In fact, we all need to recoup and revive, in a peaceful setting, in order to tackle more profoundly the events of life. Experience will quickly show you this. Further, resolving problems on a daily basis does not necessarily encourage one in spiritual progress.

Family Pilgrimages

We are part of a big family, the Church, and we all need to rediscover this dimension from time to time. The crowd, the fervor, and the spirit of sacrifice of a pilgrimage give a new momentum in our Catholic life. Without over-doing it, we ought not to neglect these days of local and national pilgrimage. They are certainly an occasion of great graces for the Church, for Tradition, and for our families. These days impose sacrifices and devotions. They are also a chance to strengthen the ties between different families of Tradition.

Human Equilibrium

The father of the family must watch over the human balance of the members of his family. This equilibrium promotes the harmonious development of both the natural and supernatural life of each member, as well as family peace and joy. This balance prevents discouragement and desolation.

Without an established order that is respected by all, peace will be difficult and virtues will be fragile.

Everyone has his limits and needs in order for his mind and body to function properly—limits and needs which he must know and respect.

Human natures are more fragile from the point of view of nerves than from a standpoint of physical stamina, so it is necessary to be aware of this reality in what you ask of or impose on others, and sometimes, more importantly, when you ask it.

Human nature has need of natural consolations and satisfactions in its activities in order to give itself more generously. This is why, after accomplishing one's duty of state, it is necessary to foresee activities agreeable to nature, without falling into caprice.

By definition, balance rests between two extremes: being too rigorous and being too lax.

Here are some areas in which the father of the family will pay special attention, with the advice and help of his wife.

Schedules

Regularity in following the schedule of rising and of going to bed serves to discipline the body and allows for a full, well-organized, and peaceful day. According to the age and health of each, it is necessary to allow from seven to nine hours of sleep. You must insist on the hour of going to bed so that in the morning the day will begin well. For children up to the age of eight, it is good to put them to bed between 8:00 and 8:30 p.m., waking them up around 7:00 or 7:30 a.m. For older children, let them stay up until 9:00 or 9:30 p.m., waking them around 6:30 or 7:00 a.m. As for the parents, do not stay up past 10:30 p.m., if possible, waking at 6:00 to 6:30 a.m.

Saturday and Sunday, you could let the children sleep a little longer to foster family harmony, taking into consideration the hour for Mass and the return to work on Monday.

The children should fall asleep right away in the evening after an edifying reading (life of a saint) to avoid impure temptations. In the morning, also, they should get out of bed right away for the same reason.

The flesh must be disciplined from childhood to better tame it in its revolts against the spirit. Caprice in this domain often has serious consequences!

A well-organized day in which the essential things are foreseen—allowing plenty of time for each activity—promotes a calm life and permits the soul to lift itself towards God.

Let us take care not to start too many things, so as not to live in a rush all the time and, therefore, to become a nervous wreck.

Of course, one must not fear to oppose idleness, which is the mother of all vices. The mother will be careful to take good care of the children, keeping them busy, especially during school vacations, assuring that the common activities are varied and suitable. This organization demands advanced planning.

Cleanliness Is Next to Godliness

Bodily Hygiene

Our body is the temple of the Holy Ghost (I Cor. 6:19), but it is also composed of rebellious flesh. This is why we have duties regarding it, so as to remain its master. These duties regard cleanliness, dignified posture, and modest attire. The child must learn to keep his clothes clean, so that they may be worn for more than one day, to keep his hair cut and combed, and not to keep his hands in his pockets. Because of original sin, the flesh rebels against the spirit to draw us into softness and laxity, disordered pleasures, and sin. This is why we must mortify our inclinations and not give in to them. It is good to avoid having the house too warm in the winter, having clothes that are too soft, taking too many showers, or having a too-relaxed posture. It is good always to wear an undershirt, to take quick showers in lukewarm water, and to get up promptly. The body should be treated with a certain asceticism, as an enemy always ready to take over our souls.

Bodily Nourishment

Eating is a matter of strengthening the body so it can fulfill its duties, not flattering all its tastes. This is why the mother will see to it that the meals are healthy, balanced, and home-made. Children must learn from a young age to eat all that is put before them.

Mealtimes are privileged moments. This is why it is necessary to plan well enough so that there is plenty of time for each to enjoy his dinner and to take part in conversation with the family. Meals are a chance to solemnize Sundays, feasts, birthdays, anniversaries, or to invite friends. The mother should prepare a meal above the ordinary on Sunday and beautify the layout of the table and the dishes.

The Rooms in the House

The mother will watch over the cleanliness and order of each room in the house. Some simple, solid furniture is sufficient. Having too many knickknacks makes it harder to keep order. Each room should be decorated simply and pleasantly.

Recreation

As much as possible, recreations should be in common. Outings and family games leave the children with the best memories and permit the strengthening of family ties.

If each evening there is a short recreation, on Sunday there should be a longer one that is varied and organized. Working in the garden, playing a musical instrument, playing little social games, or even taking time for casual conversation, constitute good evening relaxation.

As for Sunday, one could plan a picnic, a walk in the forest to identify the different trees, visiting a park to enjoy a little game, a visit with another family or with friends, or discovering an area or region researched by a member of the family. It is good to combine the pleasant, the historical, and cultural as much as possible.

Do not forget that the best family outings are those that cost little or no money. Do not allow in the home video games (which have no connection with reality), television, or games that are too costly.

Keep in mind that Sunday is meant for the family! It is not the day for the automatic nap! If the father of the family is tired, he must find other ways to spend time with the family this day.

Friends or Enemies of the Christian Home

We are social beings and are therefore influenced by the world around us. This is why it is important to reflect well upon our relations with the outside world. It can just as easily encourage us to virtue and to a healthy outlook or drive us little by little to a general relaxation in every domain.

The couple should never forget that the goal of their lives is heaven and sanctity, and that therefore they will make their choices in light of this great vocation, which the whole family shares. "Man was created to praise, reverence, and serve God, Our Lord, and by this means to save his soul."[18] They will remember that half-measures in the face of dangers to the Christian life are reprehensible because they always favor and generate lukewarmness in souls.

However, habitual constraint is not a good way to run things, either. It is necessary to know how to bring about the agreement of all, and this is done by arguments that will enlighten the understanding. It is also done by proposing and organizing other family activities that do not leave a void.

We are going to consider, firstly, the enemies of the home—the television, video games, computers, the Internet, and cell phones. We will then envision friendly family relations. Finally, we will discuss family outings.

---

[18] St. Ignatius Loyola, *The Spiritual Exercises*, Week 1.

The Screens, Enemies of the Home

The Minister of Education (in France) brought to our attention his concern in a letter sent at the beginning of 2008 to all schools:

> Our children spend just over 900 hours per year in school, but 1,200 hours in front of their computer and other screens; 96 percent of teenagers surf the Internet every day. The Internet contains numerous dangers: violent pornography, child pornography, cyber-dependence, cyber-blackmail, cyber-defamation (slander). In nearly every home there are six screens—between the TVs, computers, and game consoles.

Families are invaded now by modern means which are, on the one hand, seductive (sometimes useful), but which have incalculable evil effects for the family and for the social spirit, for moral and intellectual life, and for the balance of nature and of the home.

It is imperative to react firmly and with conviction.

Television

Television is and has been the instrument of corruption of ideas and of morals in society. It ruins family life and the spiritual life. It is an obstacle to healthy recreation and to good reading. It is a waste of precious time. It ruins education in every domain. It habituates men to live on the level of the imagination and of the feelings and in a dream world (which is recognized less and less as such).

We must not allow our hard-earned money to be wasted on this screen which is the symbol of the spirit of the world. It has no place in a Christian family!

Separate yourselves from the television in a spirit of reparation for all the evil it does and in order to set an example of what a good Catholic should be.

Keeping only a DVD player still presents a very real danger due to the increase in the number of movies available to the home and the laxity which constantly redefines what constitutes a "good movie." In principle, it is very important not to view more than one (completely healthy) movie per month, at most.

The objection that you will not be able to access information without a television is bogus. You can obtain the essential necessary news in a few minutes by radio and important current events in good newspapers. It is not a matter of being over-informed, but of being well-informed.

Electronic Video Games

Are there any children today who do not spend hours a day playing these games? In school, teachers can tell right away the serious consequences of this addiction on the part of the children—nervousness, lack of attention, no power of concentration, and no reflection. They do not live in reality, and this is very serious!

These games are in the process of destroying our youth.

Children need games that are educational, social, and physical; games that demand their attention, their reflection, their efforts, and ones that are a real source of relaxation for body and mind. Video games and virtual reality games do exactly the opposite. They rather heighten the reflexes, make the child tense and full of nervous stress! (This is not to say that virtual reality equipment does not have its place for older children or adults when learning to drive a car or fly an airplane, for example, but children have a great difficulty in distinguishing the real and unreal, especially if the line between the two is blurred from their earliest years.)

I am not even speaking of the loss of the taste for beauty, but of habituating these children to living in an imaginary world that is both unreal and ugly (and even monstrous).

Computers

Computers can be used to accomplish one's work and to get an education. If the computer is the only means to do these things, then it is necessary to take precautions to limit the time spent on it, with a specific schedule, in such a way that family life or one's personal life is not harmed. The best way to ensure this is not to work too late at night on the computer. Thus, the last moments of the evening are consecrated to family relaxation, spiritual reading, and prayer.

Of course, we ought to banish the watching of movies or the playing of computer games; if not, we easily fall into selfishness, waste precious time, and easily place ourselves in the occasion of sin.

The Internet

This is the most dangerous screen—not only by reason of the innumerable, impure provocations—but because in the use of the Internet, the subject becomes active. Curiosity frequently drives us to occasions of sin in all areas.

The Internet makes us lose the sense of the real and plunges us into intellectual paralysis and dissipation of soul. At the same time, this instrument demands a level of concentration which can sweep us away in an excitation of spirit and of nervous fatigue.

As soon as we connect to the Internet, we are fascinated by all the possibilities, and time ceases to be a factor. We also easily forget our family and our duties. It is really more mesmerizing than the television, which is bad enough.

If there is a real need to work on the Internet from time to time, it is necessary to take strict measures to avoid falling into its traps—the computer should be in a common room, in view of all. Before logging on, the parent should determine the time intended for the connection, the children must ask permission for it, and the parent must stick to his decision.

If your usage is limited to e-mail, in order not to become enslaved to this electronic mailman, send them only once or twice a week, do not stay up late doing so, and take time to reflect before responding. Matters that are truly urgent should not be dealt with on the Internet.

Family Relationships

We will consider as family relationships contact with one's parents, brothers and sisters, grandparents, and sometimes uncles, aunts, and cousins.

The Fourth Commandment imposes on us particular duties towards our parents, of which we must not lose sight—respect, support and help in their needs, and prayers.

Let us be aware that it is excellent to cultivate, as much as possible, a family spirit. It is a constant support both in life and in trials. It provides a chance to act as an effective influence on those who are tempted to abandon the Faith or good morals.

As for the married couple, relationships with relatives are to be regulated by four principles:

- Harmony between the two spouses is essential. "For this cause, a man shall leave his father and mother and shall cleave to his wife. And they two shall be in one flesh. . . . What therefore God hath joined together, let no man put asunder" (Mk. 10:7-9).

- The spiritual life must not be endangered. "And fear ye not them that kill the body and are not able to kill the soul: but rather fear him that can destroy both the soul and body in hell" (Mt. 10:28). That is to say, we should fear the one who would cause us to lose the Faith or grace little by little by bad influence.

- The duties of raising and educating the children in Christian virtues and in good example supersede any other human or familial consideration.

- Our duty to work for the conversion of others demands a certain friendly relationship with them, but certainly we must not comfort the sinner in his sin and therefore act as if it were a small matter.

With these principles, the Christian couple will be able to regulate family visits and invitations. With modernist and liberal parents, you have to limit your visits to brief ones—at their house, once a year—in order to avoid conflicts. For brothers and sisters, the visits can be spaced further apart. The question which presents itself today is to know what to do with family members who are living in sin, are divorced and remarried, or are in some other immoral situation, as well as those who are caustic towards religion or who provoke others to evil.

The response is simple—you cannot allow into the sanctuary of your home such people who are living lives so completely contrary to the education you are trying to instill in your children. It would be a scandal to your children and, therefore, an open door for them to justify such disorders later. On the other hand, if some good may come of it, you could meet such people in private and occasionally, with the agreement of your spouse.

What should be done at meal time when certain family members are living a bad life? You have to protect the children and show clearly that you disagree with the scandal. Normally, they should not be invited. They have voluntarily contracted a contagious disease and you cannot expose your children to it!

In refusing these invitations, let us always take care to explain the disorder calmly. It is not you who disturb the family, but they who live badly. Disorder does not have rights, nor do diseases. It is not those, then, who lead good lives and keep the Commandments who should take the back seat!

Let us note that each case is distinct. Therefore it is good, in order to resolve difficult questions, for the couple to unite in prayer to see what the wisest course of action is in their specific circumstance.

Men today live in a de-Christianized world which no longer has a moral compass. This is why, while protecting the family, you must not close your hearts by an excessive harshness. In the face of a family that is Christian in name only, we should be more lenient than towards a family that was practicing the Faith, that had been given everything, and has abandoned it.

Social Contacts and Relationships with Friends

We must not neglect our social contacts, namely, professional contacts with colleagues or contacts with neighbors. However, they ought to take place in general away from the home, or, at any rate, not during a meal. If a chance to influence someone well presents itself, do not hesitate to get together again, all the while being prudent.

As for relationships with friends (with the same ideals), be available for them just as much for yourself as for your children. You can do yourself a lot of good, enlarging the subjects of conversation and of experience.

All the same, make sure not to be exclusive. Your circle of friends should not be reduced to one or two families. It should not turn into a clique which little by little casts a bad light on others.

Family Outings

Vacations, sports, local festivals, parties, and movie houses or cinemas, fall under this title, but also parish activities—carnivals and bazaars, days of recollection, study groups, etc.

Vacations are for relaxing in a healthy manner and for strengthening family ties, giving everyone a chance to create good, happy memories of time spent together. Let us avoid, then, places that are occasions of sin, and organize vacations for the good of all the members of the family. Relaxation does not exclude the spiritual life, nor sufficient rest. You have to think about it and plan for it.

Sports can be a regular, praiseworthy recreation. However, be careful not to let them take away from family recreation. This is why on Sunday, as well as on vacations, you should endeavor to find a common recreation.

You ought, barring exceptions, to exempt yourself from local secular festivals. You will very quickly find yourself ill at ease in such places. If your presence is useful for social life, a short stay will permit you to make an appearance.

Movie theaters and worldly parties are forbidden. These are no longer the setting of healthy recreation or useful contacts, but near occasions of sin.

Healthy activities for the youth exist around the priories, as in vacation camps. They must be encouraged, just as having young people over to different houses in the afternoon or on weekends.

Young people need social contact, and parents must foster good friendships for them. However, they will take care to inform themselves of healthy activities in order to avoid idleness, the mother of all vices.

The priory forms a great family around the prior. In addition, the activities organized by the prior (bazaars, spiritual conferences, recollections for the young or for the newly married, the Eucharistic Crusade) have priority over other activities, to the extent that they are not too frequent. These parish activities nourish the soul and favor the unity of the faithful around the prior and the priests. This is important.

Conclusion

As Catholic couples, nourished with traditional grace and doctrine, you have a grave duty. It is to create, even at the cost of great sacrifices, a stable, unified, Christian home, which is therefore edifying and happy.

Let me summarize the points to mark out for the youth of today who have no idea of the fruits of a good Christian life: "You are the salt of the earth. But if the salt loses its savour, wherewith shall it be salted? You are the light of the world. So let your light shine before men that they may see your good works and glorify your Father who is in heaven" (Mt. 5:13-16).

The Church and society need young men and young women who are balanced, virtuous, and zealous. They can only come from good Catholic families: "Even so every good tree bringeth forth good fruit.... A good tree cannot bring forth evil fruit" (Mt. 7:17).

Finally, it is in living according to these principles—which often boil down to common sense—that you will experience the simple peace, joy, and happiness here on earth that you will hopefully know and enjoy in heaven.

Please retain a few key words from this booklet, which will be our constant slogan:

- **Order.** God is served first and each one of us in his rightful place.

- **Enjoyment of life.** To give oneself for the good of others without fear of self-sacrifice.

- **Balance** according to the human and social plan.

- **Organization** in order to have a calm and peaceful life.

- **To distinguish oneself** from the spirit of the world, from its fashions, from its suggestions, all the while living in the world.

May God bless you and help you!

Appendix: Consecration of Families to the Sacred Heart of Jesus and the Immaculate Heart of Mary

Most Sacred Hearts of Jesus and Mary, which form but one heart by Your intimate union, here we are before You to solemnly consecrate to You our hearts, so that we will be, in the example of the first followers of Christ, one heart and one soul.

You have manifested the desire to reign over homes, and You have taught us at Nazareth the ideal of family peace and happiness. In order to imitate You, we want, with Your help, to make our home:

- **a kingdom of order**, where each is in the place due to him, be it a place of commanding or of obeying;

- **a kingdom of joy**, where sincere affection, mutual understanding, and mutual aid triumph without sadness and in spite of any difficulty;

- **a kingdom of piety**, to preserve which we promise to remain faithful to the faith of our fathers and to prayer in common, especially the daily recitation of the rosary. We desire to keep all the laws of God and of the Church and to nourish our supernatural life by the frequent reception of the sacraments;

- **a kingdom of charity**, and in this goal, we want to console and assist those who are suffering. We want to carefully eradicate all spirit of criticism or of slander in our conversations;

- **a kingdom of purity**, in strictly avoiding all that could disturb this beautiful virtue;
- **a kingdom of justice**, in generously repairing our faults by voluntary penance.

We also offer You sacrifices and prayers for the conversion of sinners and for the establishment of Your reign of love in families, in nations, and in all of society.

Deign to bless our resolutions and vows, our joys and our sorrows, and our spiritual and temporal interests.

Preserve us in peace and give us, in times of trial, Christian resignation to the will of God.

Most holy Hearts of Jesus and Mary, as a sign of Your particular protection, deign to inscribe the name of each of the members of our family in Your Hearts.

We ask of St. Joseph, model of all fathers of families, to present our act of consecration to You himself, and to obtain for us from Your bounty the grace to be able, one day, to be reunited as a family in heaven. Amen.

Most holy Hearts of Jesus and Mary, make our hearts like unto Yours!